PUB STROLLS IN
WEST SUSSEX

Ben Perkins

COUNTRYSIDE BOOKS
NEWBURY BERKSHIRE

First published 2002
© Ben Perkins 2002

Revised and Updated 2007

All rights reserved.
No reproduction permitted without the prior
permission of the publisher:

COUNTRYSIDE BOOKS
3 Catherine Road
Newbury, Berkshire

To view our complete range of books,
please visit us at
www.countrysidebooks.co.uk

ISBN 1 85306 730 X

Designed by Graham Whiteman

Typeset by Techniset Typesetters, Newton-le-Willows
Produced through MRM Associates Ltd., Reading
Printed by Cambridge University Press

Contents

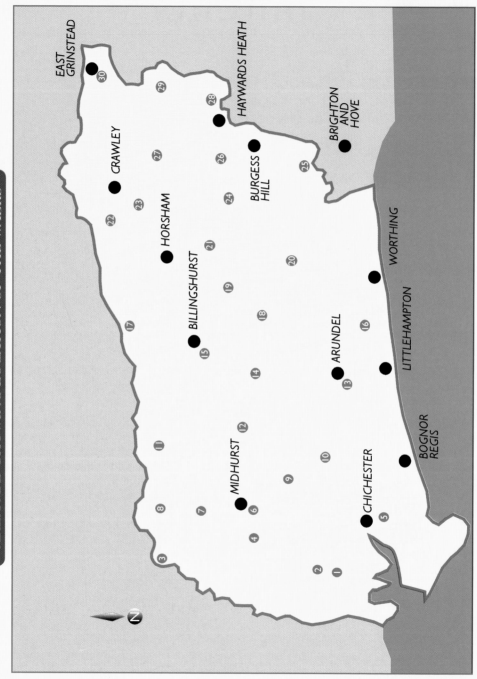

AREA MAP SHOWING LOCATION OF THE WALKS

PUBLISHER'S NOTE

We hope that you obtain considerable enjoyment from this book; great care has been taken in its preparation. Although at the time of publication all routes followed public rights of way or permitted paths, diversion orders can be made and permissions withdrawn.

We cannot, of course, be held responsible for such diversion orders and any inaccuracies in the text which result from these or any other changes to the routes nor any damage which might result from walkers trespassing on private property. We are anxious though that all details covering the walks are kept up to date and would therefore welcome information from readers which would be relevant to future editions.

The simple sketch maps that accompany the walks in this book are based on notes made by the author whilst checking out the routes on the ground. They are designed to show you how to reach the start, to point out the main features of the overall circuit and they contain a progression of numbers that relate to the paragraphs of the text.

However, for the benefit of a proper map, we do recommend that you purchase the relevant Ordnance Survey sheet covering your walk. The Ordnance Survey maps are widely available, especially through booksellers and local newsagents.

Thanks to its underlying geology, West Sussex is a county of delightfully contrasted landscapes. From the relatively featureless, though not unattractive, coastal plain, the South Downs rise in a series of folded hills and valleys, culminating abruptly in the steep northern escarpment, which can be enjoyed at its most spectacular when stepping out from Heyshott. In the north-west corner of the county is a lovely and relatively unfrequented area of sandy heath and woodland, the quality of which is recognised by its proposed inclusion in the, soon to be designated, South Downs National Park.

Large swathes of West Sussex are still in the hands of big estates where careful land management has ensured a balance of parkland, woods and agricultural fields. Towards the eastern end of the county, the countryside is slowly succumbing to the pressures of modern development, but areas of attractive well-wooded countryside remain completely unspoilt, interspersed with villages, most of which have managed to retain their character and integrity. Then there are the river valleys of the Eastern Rother, Arun and Adur. The walks in this book will enable you to sample this rich and varied landscape.

All 30 strolls are circular, starting and finishing at a friendly pub. Thankfully, in Sussex we cherish our many traditional inns where, as well as providing a wide range of good and interesting food, the importance of offering a choice of well-kept beers is still recognised. In almost all the pubs featured in these pages you will be able to enjoy a pint and a ploughman's at an unreserved table in a recognisable bar, as well as having the option of more sophisticated fare, usually in a dedicated dining area. As with my East Sussex volume in this series, I have sought out pubs which offer a welcome to walkers of all ages and provide an attractive, homely focus for a 'pub stroll'.

If you choose to leave your car in the pub car park while you walk (patrons only, of course!) please remember to ask first. Alternatively, if you opt for roadside parking do be careful not to block any exits or entrances.

These strolls, which vary in length from $2^1/_4$ to $4^1/_2$ miles, are all easily undertaken, although some are more up and down than others. Many of the routes, however, pass through relatively remote countryside. Signposting is sometimes sporadic and paths may become overgrown, particularly in late summer. Be sure to set out well shod, armed with a good map, plenty of time and your sense of adventure intact. I am sure you will then obtain the same rich enjoyment following these walks as I did.

Ben Perkins

Funtington
The Fox & Hounds

| **MAP:** OS EXPLORER 120 (GR 799083) | **WALK 1** | **DISTANCE:** $3\frac{3}{4}$ MILES |

DIRECTIONS TO START: FUNTINGTON IS ON THE B2178, LATER B2146, ROAD FROM CHICHESTER TO SOUTH HARTING, ABOUT A MILE EAST OF A LINK POINT WITH THE B2147 FROM EMSWORTH. **PARKING:** IN THE PUB CAR PARK ON THE OTHER SIDE OF THE ROAD, OPPOSITE THE PUB.

Three small communities, each within the parish of Funtington and each with a well-recommended pub, feature on this walk. Funtington itself is the largest of the three and the only one with a church, passed near the start of the walk. Although much restored, it retains a 15th century tower. The walk heads out across fields to visit the smaller settlement of West Ashling, no more than a handful of cottages grouped near an old converted mill and the associated pond, constructed in the early 19th century and now being carefully restored. Another field path takes us on to East Ashling, the smallest of the three villages. The return route loops to the north along quiet lanes and through Stoke and Ashling Woods.

The Fox & Hounds

As an old photograph on the wall of the bar testifies, the front of the Fox & Hounds looks much the same today as it did about 100 years ago. Inside, the front bar with its boarded floor and open fireplace probably hasn't changed much either. A carpeted extension for diners at the rear is newer and incorporates the well which once stood behind the pub and is now an attractive indoor feature. The dining area opens onto a walled garden.

The pub is owned by Hall and Woodhouse and serves their Badger beers, as well as a guest ale from a local brewery. The quality food menu, with dishes such as Beef and Badger Ale Pie, is all home-cooked and snacks include ploughman's and sandwiches made from granary or ciabatta bread with a wide choice of fillings.

Opening times are from 12 noon to 3 pm and 6.30 pm to 11.30 pm on Monday to Saturday, 12 noon to 4 pm on Sunday. The pub is closed on Sunday evenings. Food is served from 12 noon to 2.30 pm and 6.30 pm to 9.30 pm except Sunday evenings. Children are welcome as are dogs (in the bar only). Telephone: 01243 575246.

The Walk

① From the pub turn left along the B2146. Soon after passing the village shop on your right, go right along Church Lane. On reaching the church lychgate, bear left along a rough track which skirts to the left of the churchyard. Pass between staggered railings and head out across a large field on a well-preserved

path. Go over a metalled drive and continue on a clear field path which brings you out via a short enclosed path to a lane. Turn right and immediately fork left.

② At a road junction opposite the corner of West Ashling millpond turn left along a segregated path to the right of the road. (For the Richmond Arms turn right here. The pub is a short distance past the pond. Return the same way.) Carry on through West Ashling to a T-junction with Southbrook Road where you should turn left.

③ After about 200 yards go right along a signposted path which follows a right field edge at first. After about 400 yards this clear path veers half left across a field and brings you out between houses and on along a lane to reach the B2178 at East Ashling. Turn left and follow this road past the Horse and Groom pub on the left. Soon after passing the pub, fork right, signposted to West Stoke and Lavant.

④ After 400 yards fork left past a metal barrier into Stoke Wood. After another 250 yards go straight over the first signed crossing path and, very shortly, go left along a second wide crossing path which takes a straight course through Ashling Wood, a fine area of broadleaved

---

PLACES OF INTEREST NEARBY

About 4 miles to the south-east is **Fishbourne Roman Palace**, the excavated remains of a large Roman house, containing some impressive mosaic floors and an associated museum. It is open daily from February to December. For opening hours telephone 01243 785859 (or visit www.sussexpast.co.uk).

The millpond at West Ashling

woodland, for $^1/_2$ mile out to a lane.

⑤ Your next path starts opposite and soon heads out on a wide grassy strip flanked by two areas occupied currently by pigs. It takes you on past chicken houses and out to a lane. Turn left and follow this quiet lane back to Funtington. At the B2146 bear right, back through the village to the start.

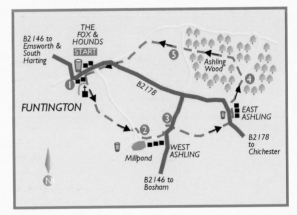

Stoughton
The Hare & Hounds

MAP: OS EXPLORER 120 (GR 803115)   **WALK 2**   **DISTANCE:** 3 MILES

DIRECTIONS TO START: STOUGHTON IS SIGNPOSTED ALONG A NARROW LANE WHICH HEADS NORTH-EASTWARDS FROM THE B2146 CHICHESTER TO SOUTH HARTING ROAD ABOUT 6 MILES OUT OF CHICHESTER. **PARKING:** THERE IS ROOM TO PARK ALONG THE LANE NEAR THE PUB.

Some of the best walking in the South Downs is to be found to the north and west of Chichester where this line of rolling hills is at its widest and most thinly populated. The tiny village of Stoughton lies surrounded by low wooded hills towards the far end of a long valley where the undulating dip slope of the Downs begins to open out towards the coastal plain. This fairly gentle stroll, involving only fairly modest ups and downs and all along well-signed paths and tracks, crosses over into the next valley and returns along a delectable path through Inholmes Wood, once threatened with destruction by clear felling but now in the safe hands of the Forestry Commission. Parts of the wood suffered badly in the Great Gale of 1987 but many fine mature beech trees withstood the ravages of the wind and natural regeneration is now well under way to fill the gaps.

The Hare & Hounds

Housed in a 350 year old building constructed from the vernacular flint so characteristic of many downland villages, the Hare & Hounds once served as both village shop and post office as well as alehouse but is now a comfortable village local with a strong emphasis on good food. Outside, during the summer months, the front of the pub is colourfully decorated with hanging baskets overlooking a paved patio and there is a garden at the rear. Inside are three cosy bar areas, each with a log fire in winter.

This privately owned free house is proud of the quality of its beer and currently there are six real ales on hand pump including Hampshire Rose Bitter from the Itchen Valley Brewery and Timothy Taylor's Landlord bitter from Yorkshire. The regularly rotated blackboard menu includes a balanced mix of old favourites such as rack of lamb as well as more adventurous specialities such as steak and pigeon pie. Sandwiches and filled rolls are also on offer as well as a good choice of substantial puddings.

Opening times are from 11am to 3pm and 6pm to 11pm on Monday to Friday, 11am to 11pm on Saturday and 12 noon to 10.30pm on Sunday. Food is served daily from 11am to 2pm and 6pm to 10pm. Children and dogs are welcome. Telephone: 02392 631433.

The Walk

① Set out on a gravel track, signed as a footpath, which starts immediately to the right of the pub. After a few yards go

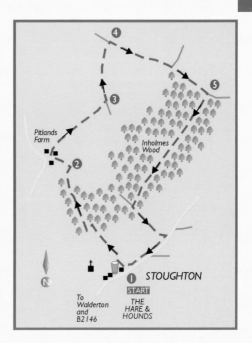

forward over a stile, ahead across a field to a second stile and up along a right field edge. On reaching an area of woodland, go left on a path within the edge of the wood for a few yards, then right over a stile and up through the wood. Go straight over two successive crossing tracks and down through a fine area of beech woodland. Go over a third crossing track and shortly leave the wood over a stile.

② Head out across a field aiming just to the left of the buildings at Pitlands Farm. On reaching the farm and about 20 yards short of a lane turn right between the farm buildings and on along a track which climbs gently at first and then contours along the side of this peaceful valley for about ¼ mile.

③ Where this track comes to an end, go ahead to an isolated fingerpost in the middle of the field where you should turn

The view back to Stoughton near the start of the walk

left. Paths should be marked out through any growing crop. At the edge of the field go ahead through a belt of trees and along the right edge of the field beyond.

④ At a T-junction with a substantial track, signposted as a bridleway, turn right. Sheltered by trees at first it then crosses more open ground with a vista to the right down the valley to the sea with the Isle of Wight in view on a clear day. The main track goes left and right, marked with a blue waymark as it enters Inholmes Wood. Ignore the track which goes off to the left along the edge of the wood and go straight over the first wide crossing track within the wood.

⑤ At a waypost turn right following a narrower path marked with a yellow arrow. It traverses an area of thinner woodland with a series of views across the valley to

PLACES OF INTEREST NEARBY

Stansted Park, a few miles to the west though accessible only indirectly by road from Stoughton, is a major tourist honey pot – a stately home set in 1,750 acres of parkland, with ancillary attractions such as a garden centre, an arboretum and a Victorian walled garden as well as a shop and tearoom. The grounds are open daily throughout the year; the house on Sunday to Wednesday, 1 pm to 5 pm, between April and October. For more details telephone 023 9241 2265.

the left towards Bow Hill. The path contours along the wooded hillside for a good $1/2$ mile. Where the path divides, keep left and, very shortly, leave the wood and go forward along the lower wood edge. At a T-junction with a wider track turn left and drop down between banks to join a lane. Turn right, back into Stoughton, a few minutes walk away.

Rake
The Two Counties Inn

MAP: OS EXPLORER 133 (GR 804278)) **WALK 3** (DISTANCE: 3½ MILES

DIRECTIONS TO START: RAKE IS ON THE B2070, PREVIOUSLY THE A3. BEST ACCESS IS FROM THE A3 AT LISS VIA THE B3006 OR FROM THE A272 AT SHEET OR ROGATE. **PARKING:** PATRONS ARE WELCOME TO USE THE PUB CAR PARK WHILE ON THE WALK BUT ASK PERMISSION FIRST.

Rake lies within an extensive area of sandy heath and woodland at the north-west corner of the county on the Hampshire/West Sussex border. The walk sets off along part of the Sussex Border Path, dropping down to follow the foot of Rake Hanger before turning east to explore an area of open access Forestry Commission woodland. Some care is needed here with navigation as some of the paths used are unsigned and not marked as rights of way on the Explorer map. It is a pleasantly sheltered stroll, probably at its best in the spring and autumn, when the leaf colour is at its finest, but good at any time of year as the well-drained sandy soil is reasonably dry underfoot in all seasons.

The Two Counties Inn

This pub, formerly known as the Flying Bull, is a relatively modern pub, dating from the 1920s and built to replace a much older hostelry, now demolished. The present building stands astride the Hampshire-Sussex boundary, so that you can stand in the bar with a foot in each county. It is a particularly walker-friendly pub, well placed for hikers along the 150 mile Sussex Border Path as well as more gentle strollers. The interior comprises a comfortable carpeted open plan bar area with a pool room at the back and outside, a patio with barbecue facilities and a shady lawn.

The Two Counties Inn is an Eldridge Pope house, run by tenants. The beers on offer include Courage and Ringwood Best bitters. The menu, regularly changed, with food prepared and cooked on the premises from fresh ingredients, might include braised steak and dumpling, as well as speciality dishes, wood-fired pizzas and snacks such as Welsh rarebit or a choice of sandwiches.

Opening times are from 11.30 am to 3 pm and 5.30 pm to 11 pm on Tuesday to Saturday, and 12 noon to 4 pm on Sunday. Food is served from 12 noon to 2.15 pm and 6 pm to 9.30 pm. The pub is closed on Sunday and Monday evenings. Children and dogs are welcome in the pub. Telephone: 01730 892285.

The Walk

① Start the walk along a lane which leaves the B2070 opposite the pub and drops downhill. At the bottom of this short slope fork right along an unmade access drive, signposted as a bridleway. Beyond the last house, Holly Cottage, a path continues along the foot of the wooded Rake Hanger for over $1/2$ mile out to a road.

② Turn right and, after less than 100 yards, double back to the left along a wide forestry track which contours along the hillside through partially cleared coniferous woodland. Ignore a downhill left fork, keeping to the higher path which continues on a fairly level route with views opening out to the left. Continue through to a road and turn left.

③ After 60 yards turn right along a well-trodden path signed as part of the Serpent Way. At a T-junction with a wide sandy track turn sharply back to the left and, where the main track bears round to the right, go ahead along a wide grassy path. Where this path, in turn, bears right, go ahead for 10 yards to join a road.

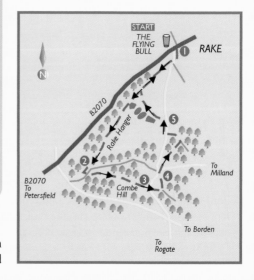

Rake Hanger

④ Go ahead over an earth barrier, opposite, over more wooden railings and ahead on a woodland path, narrow and indistinct in places. At a junction with a path coming in from the right, go ahead, dropping gently downhill. At the bottom of the hill, at a T-junction, turn left, now with a low forestry fence on your right. Follow this clear path out to a road where you must negotiate another wooden fence. Turn right.

⑤ After about 300 yards turn left over a stile and follow a fenced path across a valley, passing a series of fishing ponds, away to your left. After about 200 yards, fork half right, over a stile and across a

PLACES OF INTEREST NEARBY

About 6 miles south down the A3 is the **Queen Elizabeth Country Park**, a 1,400 acre area of woodland and chalk downland with a visitor centre, shop and café, and opportunities for walking and cycling along marked trails. The park is open throughout the year, the visitor centre from April to October and at weekends in winter. Telephone: 023 9259 5040.

field to a second stile. Go ahead to a third stile beside a gate where you will rejoin your outgoing route at the foot of Rake Hanger. Turn right and retrace your outgoing footsteps back to the start.

Elsted Marsh
The Elsted Inn

MAP: OS EXPLORER 120 (GR 834206) | **WALK 4** | **DISTANCE:** 4 MILES

DIRECTIONS TO START: FROM THE A272 ABOUT 2$\frac{1}{2}$ MILES WEST OF MIDHURST, FOLLOW AN UNCLASSIFIED ROAD SOUTH, SIGNPOSTED TO SOUTH HARTING. ELSTED MARSH IS ABOUT 2 MILES ALONG THIS ROAD. **PARKING:** IN THE PUB CAR PARK WITH PERMISSION OR A FEW YARDS ALONG THE LANE WHICH HEADS NORTH OPPOSITE THE PUB.

A first glance at the map suggests that this walk traverses an unpromising, apparently flat and featureless, agricultural landscape. However, it offers unexpected delights. The field layout is on a relatively small scale and fine mature oak trees line many of the hedgerows. Throughout the walk, which has more ups and downs than you might expect, all short and modest, you can enjoy a series of fine views of the wooded northern Downs escarpment between Treyford Hill and Beacon Hill. The walk also passes through the tiny and remote settlements of Treyford and Didling, each no more than a farm, manor house and a handful of cottages. The walk uses field paths (all rights of way), some of which may be obscured by growing crops, so care is required with navigation in one or two places.

The Elsted Inn

This was built in late Victorian times to serve the railway station on the line which once linked Midhurst with Petersfield. As the inn sign suggests, it was once the Railway Inn, being renamed well after the line was finally closed down. In private ownership until quite recently, it is now part of the Enterprise Inn chain, though it has lost none of its original character, retaining scrubbed wood floors and a generally plain interior with a separate public bar and a bright non-smoking dining area. Outside is a paved patio and lawn with a view southwards towards the tree-covered South Downs.

The beers on draught are currently Ballard's and Youngs plus Fuller's London Pride and there is a distinguished wine list. There are two separate menus. The bar snacks embrace, as well as sandwiches and jacket potatoes, some time honoured pub favourites such as cottage pie and ham, egg and chips. On a blackboard list, changed regularly, you can choose from more distinctive specialities like home-made bacon, sage and onion roly-poly pudding. Cream teas are also available.

Opening times are from 11 am to 11 pm on Monday to Saturday, 12 noon to 10.30 pm on Sunday. Food is served daily from 12 noon to 3 pm (4 pm on Sunday) and 7 pm to 9.30 pm. Dogs are welcome as are children, the latter in the restaurant area only. Telephone: 01730 813662.

The Walk

① From the pub turn left along the road. Cross the bridge over the old railway and, after 70 yards, turn left along a tree-lined path. Beyond a footbridge, head straight out across a cultivated field, walking parallel to minor power lines. The path may be indistinct after ploughing and planting. Go through a wide gap in the next hedge and on across another field.

② Go through a gate and ahead along a wide grass path between two lines of oak trees, marked as Brimbrook Lane on the Explorer map. After 350 yards turn right through a wide gap to a stile and head half left across a field, through a gap in a line of oak trees and on, without changing direction, across the field beyond. Go through another gap, across a field corner and ahead along the left field edge.

③ After 250 yards or so go left over a culvert and through a gate. Now veer slightly left across a field to cross a stile, then turn right along a right field edge, up and over a low rise. Continue along a short

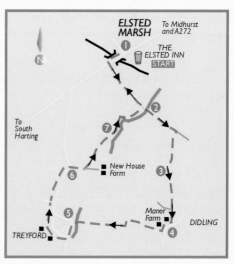

Treyford Hill

enclosed path and out via the access drive from Old Cottage to join a lane at Didling.

④ Turn right and follow this lane round a left hand bend, passing Manor Farm on the right. Just beyond the farm buildings, turn right along a concrete farm access drive. Beyond the farmyard go forward over a stile and veer slightly right down to a stile in the bottom right field corner, then uphill with a hedge, right. In the field corner the path goes left and right over two stiles and on along the right edge of one field and the left edge of the next, then down to cross a stream in an unexpected wooded dip and up and out past a cottage to join a lane.

⑤ Turn left past an attractive thatched cottage to a junction of lanes where you should turn right through the tiny hamlet of Treyford. Follow the lane north out of the village. At a road junction, go ahead, signed to Midhurst and Elsted Marsh. Follow this quiet lane as it burrows through a cutting, shaded by massive trees maintaining an apparently precarious hold on the steep roadside banks.

⑥ Where the lane emerges from this cutting, turn right along the roughly metalled drive to New House Farm. Just beyond a pair of cottages, at a waypost, turn squarely left across grass to a gate in the field corner, on in the same direction across the field beyond to another gate, then slightly right across a field to a stile in the far right corner.

⑦ Once over this stile, go forward through a gate and over a culvert, then bear half left across a meadow to go through a gate and over another culvert. Now turn right around the right field edge with a half hidden stream on your right. On reaching a crossing path, marked by a sign, you are back at point 2. Turn left and retrace your outgoing route back across two fields, on along the enclosed path to the road, then right, back to the pub.

PLACES OF INTEREST NEARBY

A few miles to the south via South Harting and the B2146 is **Uppark**, a 17th century stately home, beautifully situated deep within the South Downs. The house has recently been rebuilt following a catastrophic fire in 1989. Luckily, most of the contents, including a remarkable 18th century dolls' house, were saved from the flames. It is a National Trust property open between April and October, except on Fridays and Saturdays; the grounds, shop and restaurant from 11.30 am to 5.30 pm, the house from 1 pm to 5 pm. Telephone: 01730 825857.

Hunston
The Spotted Cow

MAP: OS EXPLORER 120 (GR 862019) | **WALK 5** | **DISTANCE:** 3 MILES

DIRECTIONS TO START: FROM THE CHICHESTER BYPASS FOLLOW THE B2145 SELSEY ROAD SOUTHWARDS FOR 2 MILES TO HUNSTON. THE SPOTTED COW IS ON THE MAIN ROAD THROUGH THE VILLAGE.
PARKING: YOU MAY PARK IN THE PUB CAR PARK WITH PERMISSION.

This walk starts out along field paths to the south and east of the village. After visiting the parish church, well away from the main settlement and surrounded by a delightful grouping of farm and manor house, we return beside an attractive section of the former Chichester Ship Canal between Crosbie Bridge and Poyntz Bridge, now a tranquil backwater. The 4 mile Chichester Ship Canal, linking the basin at Chichester with the harbour at Salterns Lock, once carried ships weighing up to 100 tons and 85 ft in length and was officially opened in 1823, together with a barge canal link to the River Arun at Ford. The village of Hunston stood at the busy junction of these two canals. The ship canal became disused in 1906 but in recent years has been partially restored for leisure craft, though not as a navigable through route.

The Spotted Cow

A large family-orientated establishment owned by Fuller's Brewery, the Spotted Cow has been extended and modernised but still retains a pub atmosphere in the front bar with its flagstone floor and low beams. A large bright and airy dining extension at the rear is furnished with modern pine tables and chairs and opens onto a covered patio. In summer you can sit out on the front lawn under colourful umbrellas or next to a children's play area at the back.

The beer is Fuller's London Pride, supplemented by Bulmers Traditional Cider on draught and the large lunch menu is all prepared and cooked on the premises. It embraces a variety of individual dishes such as home-baked pie, with changing ingredients, and slow-cooked lamb shank, all using locally-sourced produce. There are some interesting vegetarian alternatives as well as the usual sandwiches, ploughman's lunches and jacket potatoes.

Opening times are from 11 am to 3 pm and 5 pm to 11 pm (to 10.30 pm on Sunday) in summer and 12 noon to 2.30 pm and 5.30 pm to 11 pm in winter. Children and dogs are welcome. Telephone: 01243 786718.

The Walk

① From the pub turn right and, after a few yards, go left along a narrow path which tends to become overgrown. Where this short enclosed path ends go ahead along a left field edge until you can turn left over a plank bridge and go ahead with

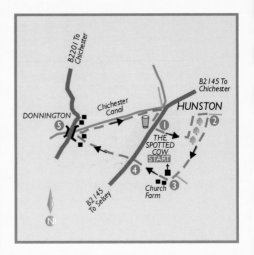

woodland on your right. In the field corner go over a stile, forward for 20 yards, then right over another stile and plank bridge and ahead, still with the wood on your right.

② After another 200 yards or so go right between staggered railings and forward along a right field edge, once again with the wood on your right (you have now walked round three sides of this small area of woodland). A good path and then a headland track take you southwards through a flat, open, fertile, intensively farmed landscape for about $\frac{1}{2}$ mile.

③ On reaching the buildings at Church Farm turn right on a path which starts between concrete bollards and a post and rail fence. After a few yards go forward along a drive to reach the tiny Hunston parish church, well separated from the village and dedicated to the obscure St Leodegar. A few yards past the church bear left across a patch of grass with a pond on your left and, after a few more yards, bear right on a clear path between a fence and ditch. Where the path ends,

Poyntz Bridge over the Chichester Canal

veer slightly left across a recreation ground to exit onto the B2145 to the left of a children's play area.

④ Turn left and, after a few yards, go right along a road called Little Boultons. Where this road bears left, go ahead along a narrower access, straight over a crossing path and forward along a right field edge. To follow the next section some care is needed as the path is unsigned and may be ploughed and planted over. After about 250 yards go right through a gap in the hedge and left along the other side of the hedge, soon diverging from it to cross a field, aiming to the right of an open sided barn. At the barn go forward along a drive, leaving the open barn on your left and a

more solid building to your right, to join the B2201.

⑤ Turn right and, after a few yards, fork right along the Chichester Canal towpath which you can now follow for over $\frac{1}{2}$ mile to reach the B2145 at Poyntz Bridge. Turn right beside this road, back to the start.

Midhurst (west of)
The Half Moon

DIRECTIONS TO START: THE HALF MOON IS SET BACK TO THE NORTH OF THE A272 ROAD TO PETERSFIELD ON THE WESTERN EDGE OF MIDHURST. **PARKING:** IN THE PUB CAR PARK WITH PERMISSION.

From a convenient starting point on the edge of the charming market town of Midhurst, well worth exploring before or after the walk, we are quickly away onto the wooded heathland of Midhurst Common. We then head north to reach the pleasant little village of Stedham where you should allow time for a short detour to visit the church and churchyard with its massive yew tree, 35 ft in circumference. After crossing the River Rother using a lovely low arched 17th century bridge, we join the riverbank as it loops to the north via Stedham Mill, a delectable spot where the water cascades over a small weir. The return route continues beside the river along the foot of the National Trust area of Woolbeding Wood and across a meadow to reach Woolbeding Bridge, another fine old stone and brick structure.

The Half Moon

This pub, originally converted from two farm cottages, was a modest local hostelry for many years. There have been major extensions but it has not lost its traditional atmosphere in that a public or 'village' bar has been retained at one end. The rest of the pub is now a spacious modern lounge bar and dining area opening out onto a large garden, once an orchard, at the rear.

The beers, changed regularly, usually include ales from the local Ballards Brewery or Goddards on the Isle of Wight. The food menu is large and varied, and includes a variety of pub favourites, as well as home-cooked 'specials' using locally sourced ingredients.

Opening times are 11 am to at least 11 pm. Food is served from 12 noon to 8.30 pm daily. Children are welcome, as are dogs in the public bar. Telephone: 01730 810263.

The Walk

NB: Although reasonably dry during the summer months, this is a walk to avoid after winter rains as it is liable to flooding.

① From the pub turn right beside the A272. You are immediately presented with three paths to the left in quick succession. Yours is the third of these which forks left as a roughly metalled access drive. Where the drive ends at a car turning circle go ahead along a woodland path. After about 60 yards, at a waypost, fork right over a low bank and along a narrower path to join another rough gravel track and bear left along it. Shortly fork left, directed by a waymark, on a wide

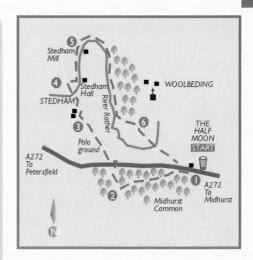

track through a conifer plantation. At a grassy clearing go ahead, passing under power lines and continuing through a wood to join a lane.

② Turn right and follow the lane until you can fork right along a signed path which descends between banks to reach the A272. Turn left and, after less than 100 yards, go right over a stile and descend through a young tree plantation and over a footbridge in a wooded dip. Cross a metalled road, go up steps and ahead across a polo ground. Cross another road and head for a white walled house where a path leads out to join a lane at Stedham.

③ Turn right and at a junction, right again. After a few yards a right fork leads to the pleasant church but the walk continues along the through road, down and over Stedham Bridge.

④ After another 200 yards or so turn right along a sandy track to a stile and then right along a right field edge, soon walking beside the river. You will shortly have a

Stedham Hall

good view of the half-timbered Stedham Hall across the water.

⑤ After about ¼ mile, when beside a weir and footbridge, turn left, away from the river, on a narrow overgrown path and, after 30 yards, go right to follow a similar path at the foot of a wooded bank. Stay next to the river on a permissive National Trust route, ignoring a left fork up the hill. Beyond a stile, keep to the left edge of a meadow, walking parallel to power lines. Go through a gate and veer half left across a field to join a lane over a stile.

⑥ Turn right and follow the lane until, just past Woolbeding Bridge, you can turn

> **PLACES OF INTEREST NEARBY**
> The town of **Midhurst**, developed on the site of a Roman crossing of the Rother, has many old timber-framed buildings. Just outside the town are the ruins of the Elizabethan **Cowdray House**, set in spacious parkland.

left along a grassy path. An enclosed path, sometimes overgrown, continues beside a field. When it opens out continue through scrub to a stile beside a gate. Beyond the stile the path officially bears right through an area of scrub but most walkers seem to use the easier alternative, ahead along a right field edge. Both routes lead out to a lane within yards of the Half Moon.

Henley
The Duke of Cumberland

| MAP: OS EXPLORER 133 (GR 894258) | WALK 7 | DISTANCE: 3 MILES |

DIRECTIONS TO START: HENLEY IS SIGNPOSTED EASTWARDS FROM THE A286 MIDHURST-HASLEMERE ROAD ABOUT 5 MILES NORTH OF MIDHURST. THE APPROACH IS ALONG A NARROW LANE, THE RECOMMENDED ROUTE BEING FROM THE NORTH ALTHOUGH THERE IS ALSO A SHORT BUT VERY NARROW LANE FROM THE A286 TO THE SOUTH OF THE VILLAGE. **PARKING:** IN THE CAR PARK WITH PRIOR PERMISSION FOR PUB PATRONS OR BESIDE THE LANE NEAR THE PUB (RESTRICTED).

The tiny settlement of Henley achieved its present tranquillity following the construction of what must have been one of the earliest bypasses, built about 1800 to ease the gradient on the main road north from Midhurst. Our walk takes an undulating route across the hilly wooded area to the east of Henley to reach the equally small hamlet of Bexleyhill, no more than a handful of cottages. It then descends northwards along an ancient trackway where you can trace the remains of the stone walls which once lined this wide road. The path opens briefly into a secluded valley formed by one of the feeder streams of the River Rother before plunging back into Verdley Wood. The final stretch involves another section of old road, gaining height to reach the pub, back on high ground with views northwards between the trees to the heights of Blackdown (see Walk 8).

The Duke of Cumberland

This lovely old pub was once a 16th century coaching inn until bypassed by the 'new' road. It now enjoys what must be one of the most idyllic settings of any pub in Sussex, hidden away on a steeply sloping wooded hillside. Fed from a spring in the woods above the pub, a tiny stream tumbles down through the 3-acre garden, over mini-waterfalls and through small constructed ponds, one of which contains trout, destined for the pub menu.

The Duke of Cumberland consists of two small unimproved rooms with tiled floors and plain wooden tables and benches. Accommodation is thus very limited, but extended on a warm summer day when everyone spills out into the garden.

The four real ales are all drawn straight from the barrel and usually include Adnams Broadside and Halfway to Heaven bitter from the local Langham's Brewery. The weekday blackboard menu is an interesting one which includes trout reared in a pond in the pub garden. The choice of snacks is also unusual with an emphasis on fish dishes such as seafood cocktail (crab and smoked fish) though it also includes ploughman's lunches and sandwiches. On Sunday the food is restricted to a Sunday roast.

Opening hours are 11 am to 11 pm on Monday to Saturday, 12 noon to 10 pm on Sunday. Food is available all through the week except on Sunday evenings and Mondays (last orders 2.30 pm and 9.30 pm). Children and dogs are welcome. Telephone: 01428 652280.

The Walk

① Set out along a gravel access drive which starts opposite the pub to the right of a telephone box. In a little over 100 yards turn left along a narrow hedged path between gardens which continues as a wider path through Verdley Wood where you should ignore all side and crossing paths until, at a Y-junction, you can fork left and immediately right, as indicated by a footpath sign. Now follow a narrower path until, at another Y-junction, you should fork right, now climbing steadily.

② At the top of the rise keep left and, after a few yards, go left again where there is another useful waypost. Continue with the main track, ignoring a signed path to the left and finally emerging onto a lane at the tiny settlement of Bexleyhill.

③ Turn left along the lane and, after 30 yards, go left again, dropping steeply down on a path, narrow at first and deeply rutted by four wheel drive vehicles in places. Further down it widens and is lined by banks and the remnants of stone walls.

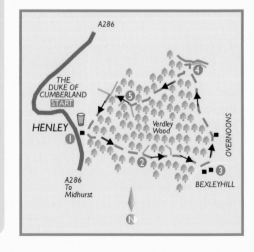

The view towards Blackdown

④ At the bottom of the hill join and go forward along a metalled drive for 30 yards only before going left along a signed path between fences. This soon turns squarely left and climbs until you can go right over a stile to plunge into dense and gloomy coniferous woodland. At the bottom of the slope go ahead over a ride and two plank bridges, then up through an area of bracken. Join and go forward along a wider track and, after about 80 yards or so, go right, still on a clear track.

⑤ At a T-junction with a wide forest track turn right and, after 100 yards or so, go ahead with the main track, ignoring a crossing path. Ignore another crossing track and, after another 60 yards, go left along a signed crossing track, now between widely spaced banks. This is another fine old road where the stone walls have been remarkably well preserved in places. It leads out via a cottage access drive to join the lane within a few yards of the pub, up the hill to your left.

> ### PLACES OF INTEREST NEARBY
> A few miles to the east via narrow lanes, at Windfallwood Common, near Lurgashall (GR 925277) is **Lurgashall Winery** where you can sample the local wines and follow a tour at weekends. Open from 9 am to 5 pm on Monday to Saturday, 11 am to 5 pm on Sunday. Telephone: 01428 707292.

Fernhurst
The Red Lion

DIRECTIONS TO START: FERNHURST IS ON THE A286 MIDHURST-HASLEMERE ROAD. THE PUB IS REACHED BY TURNING EASTWARDS ALONG CHURCH ROAD FROM THE CROSSROADS IN THE CENTRE OF THE VILLAGE. **PARKING:** IN THE RECREATION GROUND CAR PARK A FEW YARDS SOUTH OF THE PUB.

Surrounded by well-wooded hills, the pleasant village of Fernhurst nestles almost in the shadow of Blackdown, the highest hill in the county, the summit at over 900 ft being higher than any point on the Downs. Our walk keeps almost entirely within sheltered woodland, involving an easy climb onto one of the foothills of Blackdown. Although beyond the scope of this relatively short and easy circuit, the ascent of Blackdown up to the viewpoint at the Temple of the Winds is possible from point 4 on the walk, given a map and plenty of energy for the climb. This will add an extra mile as well as 300 ft of additional ascent but you will be rewarded by one of the best views in Sussex.

The Red Lion

Over 400 years old, the Red Lion has probably functioned as an alehouse for much of this time. It enjoys a lovely setting overlooking the village green and well away from the main road. Formerly a free house in private ownership it is now owned by Fuller's Brewery. The bar has a low-beamed ceiling with an inglenook fireplace and cosy dining areas at either end and there is a sheltered flower-filled garden at the rear. Dogs are welcome as are children in the dining areas.

The beers on hand pump are Fuller's London Pride, ESB and a regularly changed guest beer. The top quality home-cooked menu offers several interesting dishes such as Poacher's Casserole containing local rabbit, venison and pheasant, and 'light bites' on offer including crisy bacon and brie salad. The mouth-watering pudding menu varies but can include orange and sultana pudding and blackberry syllabub. Bar snacks (ploughman's lunches or sandwiches with unusual fillings such as Croque Monsieur) are available at lunchtime on weekdays.

Opening times are 11 am to 3 pm and 5 pm to 11 pm on Monday to Saturday, 12 noon to 3 pm and 7 pm to 10.30 pm on Sunday. Food is served daily during opening hours. Telephone: 01428 653304.

The Walk

① From the pub turn right along the lane. After about 300 yards, as the lane curves round to the left, you should fork right along a metalled drive which soon narrows to a path. Beyond a stile the path continues, enclosed, along a left field edge. Cross a drive and continue along the right edge of the next field, following a line of fine old oak trees, with a good view across the valley to your right towards the wooded heights of Blackdown. Keep to the right of the next field also to join a lane and bear right along it (almost straight ahead). Just short of a small pond on your left, fork right along a grassy track which skirts to the right of a garden and continues as a rough track signed as a public right of way.

② Shortly go right over a stile beside a gate and follow a track fairly steeply down into a valley, then left and right and up again. Where the enclosed track ends bear half right across a parking area and up a grassy bank to a T-junction with a signed bridleway and turn right. Follow this clear wide track, ignoring side and crossing paths and passing through a young tree plantation.

③ At a Y-junction where you have a choice of signed footpath or bridleway keep left with the bridleway, now entering more

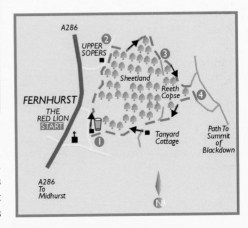

The village green, Fernhurst

mature woodland. At a T-junction of bridleways turn right and continue to reach a third junction with a metalled drive and, in front of you, a large house.

④ *For the optional extension to the summit of Blackdown, go left here, follow the drive out to a lane, turn right and after a few yards, fork left along a bridleway which leads to the summit. Return the same way.*

To complete the walk, turn right at point 4. After a few yards the path continues as a narrow path between banks, descending through woodland. Go straight over three crossing paths. Just short of the point where the path joins a lane, turn right along a woodland path which continues down with a tiny stream

in a cleft to your right. The stream passes under the path and continues down now within a deeper gorge. The path shortly heads west, soon within a wooded strip with fields on both sides. It crosses another deeply cut stream and continues past a recreation ground, back to Fernhurst.

PLACES OF INTEREST NEARBY

The Hollycombe Steam Collection can be found near Liphook, within reach of Fernhurst along narrow lanes to the west. It incorporates an Edwardian fairground plus various steam-driven devices such as traction engines and railways. It is open on Sundays and bank holidays from April to mid-October. Telephone: 01428 724900.

Heyshott
The Unicorn Inn

MAP: OS EXPLORER 120 (GR 898179), WITH A SHORT SECTION ON 121

WALK 9

DISTANCE: 3 MILES

DIRECTIONS TO START: FROM THE A286 CHICHESTER-MIDHURST ROAD ABOUT 2 MILES SOUTH OF MIDHURST, FOLLOW AN UNCLASSIFIED ROAD EASTWARDS. TURN RIGHT AT HEYSHOTT GREEN AND FORK LEFT BY HEYSHOTT CHURCH. THE PUB IS ON YOUR RIGHT A SHORT DISTANCE ALONG THE LANE.
PARKING: PUB PATRONS MAY PARK IN THE PUB CAR PARK WITH PRIOR PERMISSION. THERE IS ALSO SOME NEARBY ROADSIDE PARKING.

The steep slopes of Heyshott Down, explored on this walk, are part of a nature reserve covering an extensive area of the northern Downs escarpment. The reserve is leased by the Murray Downland Trust, and managed using selective scrub clearance and grazing to gradually restore and recreate a rich chalk downland habitat.

The walk is a fairly strenuous one which takes you up to the summit of the Downs and down again, partly along paths which have been specially constructed within the reserve for easier public access and are not marked on the OS map. The effort of the climb is rewarded by the views which open out northwards across the Weald at various vantage points, particularly during the steep and winding descent through an area of old chalk quarry workings where some care and sure-footedness is needed.

The Unicorn Inn

With its low-beamed ceiling, exposed brick walls and inglenook fireplace in which a fire is kept alight day and night during the winter months, the cosy L-shaped bar at the Unicorn has all the warmth and atmosphere you expect from an old country pub and records show that it has been an alehouse since the early 18th century. It is now a free house with quite a reputation for excellent food, offering a wide choice from bar snacks (ploughman's lunches and filled baguettes, served only in the bar) to pub staples such as steak and kidney pudding and 'specials' such as devilled kidneys, salmon fishcakes or pork tenderloin. The real ales on offer include W.J. King's Horsham Best and Timothy Taylor Landlord.

The pub has a large garden at the rear with views to the Downs and welcomes well-behaved children and dogs.

Opening times are 11.30 am to 3 pm and 7 pm to 11 pm from Tuesday to Saturday, 12 noon to 4 pm on Sunday (closed Sunday evening and all day Monday). Food is served from 12 noon to 2 pm and 7 pm to 9 pm. Telephone: 01730 813486.

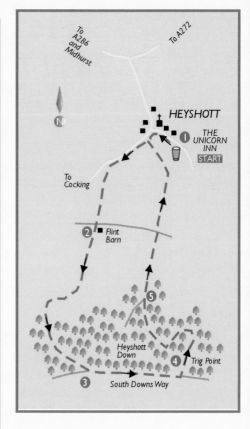

The Walk

① From the pub turn left and, at a road junction opposite the church, turn sharply back to the left along another lane. About 150 yards beyond the last house on the right, fork left through a wide gap in the hedge and head for the Downs across a large arable field where a path should be marked out through any growing crop. On the other side of the field go straight over a crossing track and ahead on another track between high hedges.

② Just past a flint barn on your left, where the track divides into two, go straight ahead between the two tracks on a narrow path which burrows into scrub and begins to climb gently between low tree-lined banks. After about 300 yards, at a waypost, turn right on a narrow path which climbs more steeply through pleasant beech and yew woodland. At the top of the wood, go over a stile and bear half left, following the direction of a yellow arrow, across a field to join a wide track.

On Heyshott Down

③ Turn left along this track, part of the South Downs Way. After a little over $\frac{1}{4}$ mile, turn left over a stile and head out across a field passing a trig point, beyond which a magnificent view to the north suddenly reveals itself.

④ Go over a stile into the Heyshott Down Nature Reserve from which a path drops steeply down the scarp slope. A short constructed zigzag eases the gradient down onto a small grassy plateau. Turn left here along a narrow path which contours along the slope, crossing two stiles in fences. About 10 yards beyond the second stile fork right downhill to cross a third stile, in sight. Turn left along a clear path with a fence on the left. A stile on the left leads into another cleared area of the reserve, worth a detour if time permits, but the walk continues ahead with the fence still on the left.

⑤ Go through a bridle gate, forward for a few yards to leave the reserve over a stile, then ahead, downhill, on a grassy, hedged path. At a crossing track go left and, after a few yards, right down steps and forward across a large field. Towards the other side of the field, join and follow a hedge, right. Go through a gap and over a plank bridge a few yards to the left of the field corner and follow the right edge of the next field round and out to the lane at Heyshott. Turn right and right again opposite the church, back to the pub.

PLACES OF INTEREST NEARBY

Both **Petworth House** (for details see Walk 12) and the **Weald and Downland Open Air Museum** at Singleton (for details see Walk 10) are within a reasonable distance. Less well known in Petworth is the **Petworth Cottage Museum**, a cottage furnished as it was when occupied by a Leconfield estate worker in 1910 (open April to October, Wednesday to Sunday, 2 pm to 4.30 pm). Telephone: 01798 342100.

East Dean
The Star and Garter

DIRECTIONS TO START: FROM THE A286 MIDHURST-CHICHESTER ROAD AT SINGLETON, HEAD EASTWARDS ALONG THE LAVANT VALLEY, PASSING CHARLTON TO REACH EAST DEAN. ALTERNATIVELY, ACCESS IS POSSIBLE WESTWARDS FROM THE A285 PETWORTH-CHICHESTER ROAD. **PARKING:** ROADSIDE PARKING IN THE VICINITY OF THE PUB.

Deep in the heart of the West Sussex Downs, the quiet and unspoilt village of East Dean is tucked away at the upper end of the valley of the River Lavant, a winterbourne stream, dry in summer, but liable to dramatic flooding during a wet winter when the footpath across the valley can become temporarily impassable. The village, built largely of flint, consists of little more than a cluster of church, pub, farm and a handful of cottages gathered round the small village green and pond. The walk climbs up onto North Down above the village with fine views to Levin Down and St Roche's Hill, before circling north to enter Charlton Forest, an extensive area of woodland covering much of the dip slope of the Downs in this area.

The Star and Garter

Previously the Hurdlemakers for a time (as shown opposite) the pub has now reverted to its original name. Its previous name was derived from a local craft which thrived in the village in the early years of the last century. It is housed in a solid foursquare two-storey flint building dating from 1750. The spacious bar opens onto a small area reserved for diners. At the rear are a patio and garden and a cottage available for self-catering holidays. It is a free house in private ownership, offering Arundel Castle Ale from the small Arundel Brewery, Adnams Best Bitter and the strong Nyewood Gold also locally produced by Ballards and served straight from the cask. The main menu concentrates on sea food and game dishes. At lunchtime you can choose from a range of snacks and more traditional pub fare. Children are welcome and dogs are allowed in the bar.

Opening times are 11 am to 3 pm and 6 pm to 11 pm on Monday to Friday, 11 am to 11 pm on Saturday, 12 noon to 10 pm on Sunday. Food is served from 12 noon to 2.15 pm and 6.30 pm to 9.15 pm daily. Telephone: 01243 811318.

The Walk

① From the front door of the pub turn right along the lane. After about 250 yards, fork left up the grassy path to the church, a picturesque approach to this lovely little flint building. Walk round to the right of the church, go right through the church car park and left, uphill, along a chalk and flint track.

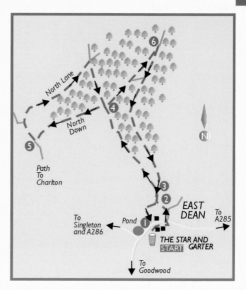

② About 50 yards after you emerge onto open downland fork right at a waypost along a grassy track between low banks which curves right and climbs to a stile beside a gate. Continue between fences.

③ Immediately beyond a bridle gate, fork left on a path which climbs across the middle of a field, indistinct but usually trodden out through any arable crop. There are two blocks of woodland in front of you and the path aims for the left end of the right hand block from which a headland path continues along the field edge with these trees on your right. Soon after the field margin bends round to the left, go right on a clear path through the wood.

④ At a signposted crossing track turn left. Leave the wood over a stile and continue in the same direction across a field with the scrub-covered slope and tree clump on Levin Down as a marker ahead. The path is indicated by a wooden post. Beyond a stile on the

East Dean

other side of the field continue down across pasture, descending more steeply over two stiles to join a farm track along the valley floor.

⑤ Turn right along this track, marked as North Lane on the Explorer map, and follow it for over ¹/₂ mile along the valley, ignoring a signed bridleway along a track to the left. Just short of a metal barrier, turn right, climbing through woodland. At a T-junction with a wide track, turn right and immediately fork left, resuming your previous direction and continuing to climb steadily. Go

PLACES OF INTEREST NEARBY

A few miles along the valley to the west, at Singleton, is the **Weald and Downland Open Air Museum** where about 40 historic buildings have been dismantled from their original sites and painstakingly re-erected within the museum grounds. It is open daily from March to October, 10.30 am to 6 pm, and in winter on Wednesdays and weekends only from 10.30 am to 4 pm. Telephone: 01243 811348.

straight over another crossing track and, after less than 100 yards you will find yourself back at point 4.

Turn left and, after about 400 yards, fork left, following the direction of a yellow arrow on a waypost (a right fork here provides a well-used short cut link to the return bridleway but is not an official right of way).

⑥ At another junction of tracks turn sharply back to the right, now on a waymarked bridleway, indicated with a blue arrow. Go over a crossing track where the previously mentioned short cut joins from the right. The track now contours along the side of an attractive beech hanger and on along a clear headland path which brings you back to the bridle gate at point 3. Retrace your outgoing route to point 2. From this point, just after you rejoin the chalk track, turn sharply right over a stile and along a left field edge until you can go left over another stile, down across pasture to a third stile and then half right down to join a lane. Go right, back to the start.

Northchapel
The Half Moon

DIRECTIONS TO START: NORTHCHAPEL IS ON THE A283 ROAD ABOUT 5 MILES NORTH OF PETWORTH AND THE HALF MOON PUB IS ON THE WEST SIDE OF THE ROAD IN THE CENTRE OF THE VILLAGE. **PARKING:** IN THE PUB CAR PARK WITH PERMISSION.

Northchapel is the only substantial community in a large thinly populated area to the east of Blackdown and within a few miles of the Surrey border. It occupies a charming landscape of modest scale, with small fields interspersed with patches of woodland, often of ancient origin. The area was once a centre of the Wealden iron industry of which traces remain in the form of a furnace pond on nearby Ebernoe Common (see Places of Interest Nearby).

This short and easy walk to the east of the village follows a pleasant mix of field and woodland paths.

The Half Moon

Once a coaching inn, the Half Moon is now a typical village 'local' with an oak beamed bar, a cosy dining area and a delightful sheltered patio and lawn at the rear. The interior is decorated with a large and idiosyncratic collection of artefacts ranging from farm implements to blow torches, gas masks and a ferret box! An inscribed board beside the bar fireplace commemorates an 18th century landlord, Noah Mann, who was also a cricketer renowned for his underarm swerve ball deliveries. He met an untimely death at the age of 33 when he fell into the pub fire after a heavy drinking session.

The present landlord of this welcoming free house offers locally brewed beers on hand pump, for example A.J. King's Horsham Bitter and Ringwood Best. The varied food menu ranges from sandwiches, soup or ploughman's lunches to more substantial dishes like steak and kidney pie, Texas chilli and local sausages. Children are allowed into the dining area and dogs are welcome in the bar.

Opening times are 12 noon to 3 pm and 6 pm to 11 pm on weekdays and 12 noon to 3 pm and 7 pm to 10.30 pm on Sundays. Food is served from 12 noon to 2 pm and 7 pm to 9.30 pm daily. Telephone: 01428 707270.

The Walk

NB: Be prepared for mud underfoot in places, particularly on the designated bridleways in Wet Wood.

① From the pub cross the road and start

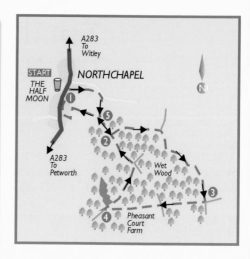

the walk along the drive to the church, signposted as a public footpath. Skirt to the right of the church, go through a kissing gate, forward within a grassy strip to a stile and on along the left edge of two fields. In the second field where the fence on your left turns away to the left, go ahead to a stile leading out to a lane. Turn right and immediately fork right along a gravel farm access drive. Where the track divides into three, keep left, signed as a public bridleway, to enter woodland.

② After about 200 yards turn left on a narrower woodland path, immediately ignoring a right fork. Once out of the wood go ahead along a left field edge. In the field corner re-enter woodland, go straight over a crossing bridleway and forward on a path which drops gently down through a pine plantation. At a path junction fork left, leave the wood through a gate, go forward for 20 yards, side step right across a culvert and resume your previous direction with a ditch and subsequently a hedge on your left. In the field corner cross a stile beside a gate

Northchapel church

and follow a right field edge with woodland to your right.

③ In the next field corner go over a stile and immediately turn right along a metalled farm drive. Follow this drive past a grove of young poplars and on, soon with a view ahead towards Blackdown. Continue with the drive past the buildings at Pheasant Court Farm and its delightful attendant pond.

④ After another 250 yards or so double back to the right along a wide track. Cross a dam at the head of a lake and continue along a wide track through Burrells Wood, a pleasant mix of oak, beech, sweet chestnut, silver birch and an occasional Scots pine. At a four-arm signpost turn left along a crossing bridleway. Back at point 2 go ahead, retracing your outgoing route for a short distance.

⑤ At the edge of the wood turn left through the second of two gates and go ahead along a right field edge with Blackdown now directly ahead. In the field corner follow the field edge round to the left. Ignore the first stile on your right which is private. Shortly go right over a second stile and along a short enclosed path out to the road at Northchapel. Turn right, back to the start.

PLACES OF INTEREST NEARBY

Accessible either by a 2 mile extension to the walk or after a short car journey from Northchapel you can explore **Ebernoe Common**, a Sussex Wildlife Trust nature reserve to the south-east of the village. It covers nearly 200 acres of ancient woodland and grassy cleared areas, supporting over 300 plant species. Park near the tiny isolated church at GR 975278.

Byworth
The Black Horse Inn

MAP: OS EXPLORER 133 (GR 987211) **WALK 12** **DISTANCE:** 3 MILES

DIRECTIONS TO START: BYWORTH IS SIGNPOSTED SOUTHWARDS FROM THE A283 ABOUT A MILE EAST OF PETWORTH. THE PUB IS ABOUT 200 YARDS ALONG THIS NARROW LANE. **PARKING:** IN THE PUB CAR PARK IF ALSO PATRONISING THE PUB. THERE IS VERY LIMITED PARKING ALONG THE LANE NEAR THE PUB.

From the tiny hamlet of Byworth, tucked away down a narrow lane, our walk climbs steadily to high ground with commanding views of Petworth and south to the ridge of the Downs. It then drops down through a lovely valley and up again to reach the edge of Petworth. From here (point 4) a short extension takes you into the Market Square at the centre of the town or to Petworth House and deer park (see Places of Interest Nearby). The return route descends again to follow the floor of another sheltered valley and back to Byworth. It is a fairly hilly route but the effort is amply repaid by the exceptional views and the variety of scenery.

The Black Horse Inn

This lovely old pub dates from 1791 though the striking three-storey classical style brick frontage was added a little later. It is full of atmosphere, with a striking interior. The front bar leads through to a series of cosy dining areas all with scrubbed wooden floors and tables with stools or bench seats. Up a steep flight of stairs at the back of the pub is a small additional restaurant area with exposed roof beams and a window with views southwards to the wooded ridge of the Downs. From a paved patio the large garden descends in a series of grassy terraces to a large lawn at the bottom.

The landlord of this free house normally has four real ales on the go, usually including Timothy Taylor Landlord and Fuller's London Pride. The food menu is an exceptional one, offering a good range of snacks. There are five different ploughman's lunches, including Dorset Stilton and Prawn Marie Rose. The main blackboard menu offers a wide choice of starters, main courses and puddings.

Opening times are 11 am to 11 pm on Monday to Saturday, 12 noon to 10.30 pm on Sunday. Food is served daily until 9.30 pm. Children and dogs are welcome. Telephone: 01798 342424.

The Walk

① From the pub turn right along the lane. After about 200 yards go left through a gate, forward to a stile and then half right up across a meadow to join the A283 over a stile beside a gate. Cross the road, go right beside it for 30 yards, then left over a stile

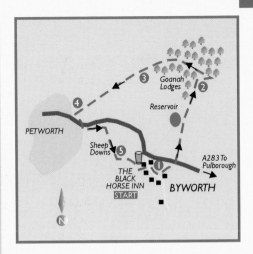

and squarely ahead across a large field. Aim for a solitary tree, continue to a stile and on in the same direction now along a headland track which passes to the left of a group of barns. Pause to look back over a wide downland panorama with a view of the escarpment between Harting Down and the Arun gap. Go over a stile beside a gate and forward along a track.

② At a crossing track with an old estate gateway and lodge to your left (Goanah Lodges) framing a distant view of Petworth House, turn right. After about 100 yards, double sharply back to the left, still on a wide track. Where the main track bears away to the right, go ahead. Continue straight over a crossing track and ahead through woodland, ignoring side paths until you can fork left between staggered railings and follow a narrow path down through scrub, soon between wooded banks. Emerge from the enclosed path at a stile and go ahead across pasture, passing to the left of an isolated tree clump. Join and go forward along an unfenced path which leads to a stile.

The path to Petworth

③ Drop downhill with a fence on your right and a fine view across the valley to Petworth House and the church. At a wooden post where you have a choice of waymarked paths, veer slightly left down across parkland to join and follow a line of stately oak trees, keeping these trees on your right. At the bottom of the hill go over a charming little brick bridge and climb steeply on a well-trodden path.

④ Go through a swing gate and turn sharply back to the left on a level path between a stone wall and post and rail fence which takes you out to the A283. Cross the road with care, turn left beside it and, after a few yards, fork right along a gravel track. Where this track bears left down to a new house you should go ahead through a swing gate. After 60 yards, at a waypost, fork left, dropping obliquely down the bracken-covered slope of Sheep Downs.

> ### PLACES OF INTEREST NEARBY
> **Petworth House** is a grand 17th century mansion set in a spacious deer park designed by 'Capability' Brown. It is a National Trust property open from April to October except Thursday and Friday. The park is open daily all the year round from 8 am to sunset. Telephone: 01798 342207. The nearby town of **Petworth** boasts a fine town hall of 1793 and a **Cottage Museum** in the form of a furnished estate worker's cottage of 1910.

⑤ Go forward through a kissing gate into woodland. After 40 yards fork left down to a rustic bridge. Go up four concrete steps, right over a stile and along a right field edge. In the field corner go right over another stile and along a narrow overgrown path which takes you out via a gravel access drive to join the lane at Byworth. The pub is now a few yards along the lane to the left.

Arundel
The St Mary's Gate Inn

MAP: OS EXPLORER 121 (GR 014072)   WALK 13   DISTANCE: 2½ OR 3¾ MILES

DIRECTIONS TO START: ARUNDEL IS ON THE A27 HALFWAY BETWEEN WORTHING AND CHICHESTER.
THE ST MARY'S GATE INN IS AT THE TOP OF THE TOWN, NEXT TO THE ROMAN CATHOLIC CATHEDRAL.
PARKING: THE PUB HAS A SMALL CAR PARK WHICH PATRONS MAY USE WHILE ON THE WALK.
ALTERNATIVELY THERE IS NORMALLY ROOM TO PARK BESIDE THE ROAD OPPOSITE THE PUB.
IF THERE IS NO SPACE HERE EITHER, PARK IN THE LARGE MILL ROAD CAR PARK AT THE
BOTTOM OF THE TOWN (POINT 5) OPPOSITE THE CASTLE ENTRANCE.

Arundel Park covers 1,200 acres of rolling downland to the north of the town and is open to the public daily except on 24th March each year. Our walk enters the park through the main entrance and crosses high open ground before dropping down to Swanbourne Lake, fed by underwater springs and a popular spot for tourists, with picnic area, tearooms and rowing boats for hire during the summer months. The full walk then takes a wide loop along the Arun riverbank back to Arundel followed by a short climb back up through the town to the start.

The St Mary's Gate Inn

Well away from the main tourist centre of Arundel, the inn can be found in the shadow of the vast Roman Catholic cathedral which, with the castle, dominates the town. Built in 1525 as a farm dwelling, the St Mary's Gate has served ale at least since the early 18th century. Inside, the spacious bar is subdivided into four areas, including one reserved for diners and a small back room – with open fireplace – opening onto a sheltered terrace garden at the rear.

The St Mary's Gate is a Hall and Woodhouse pub, offering overnight accommodation as well as food and Badger First Gold and Festive Feasant on draught. The good quality standard pub menu includes the usual steaks and grills as well as ploughman's, jacket potatoes and a choice of sandwiches at lunchtime. Regularly changed blackboard specials include more sophisticated fare such as venison casserole or lamb shank in red wine and rosemary sauce.

Opening hours are from 11 am to 11 pm on weekdays and 12 noon to 10.30 pm on Sundays. Food is served from 12 noon to 2.30 pm and 6 pm to 9.30 pm daily. Telephone: 01903 883145.

The Walk

① From the pub turn left beside the road until you can fork right through the main gateway into Arundel Park. Go ahead along a metalled drive, ignoring all side turnings. After almost $^1/_2$ mile, at a waypost, turn squarely right across grass, passing about 60 yards to the right of the

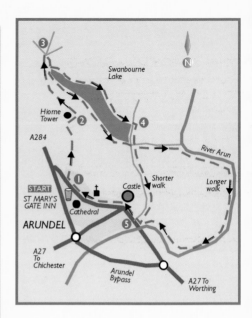

Hiorne Tower, a triangular building with castellated towers at each corner, built in 1790. Go over a gallop and ahead on a narrow path which begins to drop down.

② After 40 yards, turn left through a gateway to follow a rutted track which soon begins to lose height as it drops obliquely down the side of a beautiful downland valley.

PLACES OF INTEREST NEARBY
The town of Arundel is rich in historic and tourist attractions, including the 500 year old **Arundel Castle**, open daily except Saturday between April and October, 12 noon to 5 pm, and the **Arundel Museum** in the High Street. The **Wildfowl and Wetland Trust**, further along Mill Road beyond Swanbourne Lake, open daily from 9.30 am, summer and winter, is home to a wide variety of waterbird species, some rare and endangered. For more details telephone the Tourist Information Centre: 01903 882268.

Arundel Castle seen from the River Arun

③ At the bottom of the hill where inviting paths branch out in various directions, any of which can be explored if time permits, you should turn sharply back to the right along the floor of the valley. On reaching a stile beside a gate at the near end of Swanbourne Lake, you have a choice of paths on either side of the water. Both are a delight, particularly out of the tourist season. The main track ahead along the left side of the lake passes a refreshment kiosk and tearooms (seasonal). A right turn provides a quieter and shadier alternative along the right hand side of the lake. Both bring you out onto Mill Road where you should turn right.

④ Just short of a stone bridge carrying the road over the outflow from Swanbourne Lake, fork left on a path and cross a footbridge, parallel and to the left of the road bridge. On the other side of this bridge you have another choice. For the shorter walk go ahead along a path beside Mill Road, directly to point 5. For the longer walk, turn left beside the overgrown watercourse to your left. On reaching the River Arun, turn right and follow the raised riverbank for just over a mile back to Arundel with fine views of the castle all the way.

⑤ On reaching the road at a mini roundabout at the bottom of the town follow the main High Street up through the town. Bear right at a road junction, beneath the castle walls, then continue past the parish church and the cathedral, back to the pub.

Stopham
The White Hart

DIRECTIONS TO START: THE WHITE HART IS SIGNPOSTED SOUTHWARDS FROM THE A283 PETWORTH-PULBOROUGH ROAD ABOUT A MILE WEST OF PULBOROUGH AND JUST TO THE EAST OF THE NEW ARUN RIVER BRIDGE. **PARKING:** IN THE PUB CAR PARK WITH PRIOR PERMISSION OR BESIDE THE APPROACH ROAD TO THE PUB.

Starting across low-lying water meadows near the confluence of the River Arun and its main tributary, the Eastern River Rother, this walk follows a path along a section of the disused railway which once linked Pulborough with Petworth and Midhurst. From Lower Fittleworth, where there is another pub, the walk climbs to higher ground where it crosses Fittleworth Common, a patch of heathy woodland, returning through the tiny settlement of Stopham, past the church of Norman origins. To reach the pub again you must cross the old and beautiful Stopham Bridge, built in 1309 and now protected from further damage following diversion of the main road to the new bridge nearby.

The White Hart

Following the construction of a new bridge for the A283, the White Hart now enjoys a tranquil setting at the end of a cul-de-sac next to the lovely Stopham Bridge. The core of the pub building is probably as old as the bridge and has been selling ale to travellers on the original east-west road since 1500.

The White Hart incorporates bars on two levels, complete with cosy alcoves and an open fireplace in the lower bar plus a dining area. There is a sheltered garden opposite the pub, nestling in a curve of the River Arun. It is an Enterprise Inn offering interesting beers from local sources, including Arundel Brewery and a variety of seasonal ales from Westons Brewery at Dorking.

Separate balckboard menus offer a good choice of meat, fish and vegetarian dishes including, on my visit, lamb shank braised in honey, rosemary and garlic, peppered shark steak with spicy tomato salsa and Stilton and mushroom pasta. Bar snacks include filled baps, baguettes and jacket potatoes.

Opening times are from 10 am to 11 pm (10.30 pm on Sunday). Food is served all day, including breakfasts from 10 am to 12 noon, main meals at lunchtime and in the evening and bar snacks from 12 noon onwards. Telephone: 01798 873321.

The Walk

NB: This walk is best kept for the summer months as a section of the path on the early part of the route gets very boggy during the winter. Even in summer it can remain a little wet so walking boots are recommended.

① From the pub turn left and walk along the pub access road, once a loop of the main road, out to join the new A283. Turn right beside it and, after a few yards, opposite the entrance to a garden centre, turn right through a swing gate and bear half left on a grassy path which leads to a footbridge over the River Arun. Now veer half left across a meadow to another swing gate and on across a river bridge, this time over the Rother. Go forward along a drive passing to the right of a large water pumping station.

② About 100 yards short of a railway crossing turn right along a concrete drive. Just before reaching a building, fork left along a rough track. The track veers right to follow the line of the old railway, soon entering a section of path established for public access under the Countryside Stewardship Scheme.

③ After the best part of a mile along this track, go through a gate, forward for 20 yards then right over a stile. An enclosed path continues to a stile, where you

PLACES OF INTEREST NEARBY

To the south of Pulborough, signed from the A283, is the **Pulborough Brooks RSPB Nature Reserve**, with a visitor centre housed in a restored barn and incorporating shop, information display and tearooms. You can follow a nature trail and visit bird hides. The centre is open every day except Christmas Day and Boxing Day from 10 am to 5 pm. Telephone: 01798 875851.

should veer slightly right across a field joining the hedgerow on your right.

④ Go through a gate in this hedge, across a field corner to a stile, on through woodland and along a winding overgrown path which joins and follows the Rother riverbank through a neglected meadow for over ¹/₂ mile to join the B2138.

⑤ Turn right over the river and another bridge. A few yards short of the Swan Inn turn right along a gravel drive signed as a public footpath. Go through a gate and, after a little over 100 yards, left over a stile, up a bank, and ahead round two sides of a field with another bank on your left after you have turned the corner. Follow the field edge left and subsequently right along the lower edge of woodland. After less than 100 yards go left over two stiles and uphill with the wood on your left. In the next field corner go forward over a stile and plank bridge to join a drive and turn right.

⑥ After a few yards go left on a path which climbs across Fittleworth Common, an area of patchy wood and heathland. At a T-junction of paths turn right and after a few yards, keep right along a path which takes you out to join the A283. Turn left beside this busy vergeless road, walking on the right to face the oncoming traffic. After 100 yards go right over a stile and immediately right again on a narrow path which winds through a wooded gully. At a waypost turn left up a bank. Continue on a path within the right edge of woodland.

⑦ At a path junction bear right with an old quarry area on your left. Join and go forward along a wider track and then ahead along a lane. At a road junction turn right, soon passing Stopham church, set back across the green to your left. Continue out to the A283 and turn left. This time there is a good pavement. As you approach the new Rother bridge, fork right along a tarmac path which crosses the drive to Stopham House and continues over the old Stopham Bridge, back to the pub.

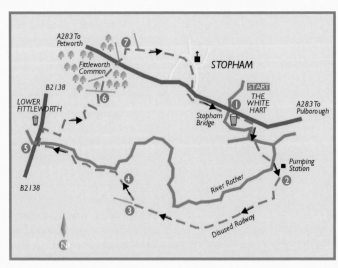

Billingshurst (west of)
The Limeburners

MAP: OS EXPLORER 134 (GR 072254)   **WALK 15**   **DISTANCE:** 3 MILES

DIRECTIONS TO START: FROM THE A272 ABOUT A MILE WEST OF BILLINGSHURST, TURN SOUTHWARDS ALONG THE B2133 TOWARDS ADVERSANE. THE PUB IS ABOUT 100 YARDS ALONG THE ROAD ON THE LEFT. **PARKING:** PATRONS ARE WELCOME TO USE THE PUB CAR PARK WHILE ON THE WALK.

The highlight of this easy walk in the Low Weald is a stroll for just over a mile along a partially restored section of the Wey and Arun Junction Canal. This waterway, dubbed 'London's Lost Route to the Sea', once wound for almost 20 miles across the Weald, linking the River Wey at Godalming with the River Arun at Pallingham, only a few miles south of where we join the canal. On the walk we pass Newbridge, once a busy wharf and the site of the original Limeburners. Further north we visit Rowner Lock, one of the first of the locks to be restored by the Wey and Arun Canal Society, an energetic organisation dedicated to restoring the canal as a navigable route. For the time being you can sample the canal on foot using the Wey-South Path, which follows the line of the canal as closely as public rights of way allow.

The Limeburners

The original Limeburners was licensed in 1805 and stood by the canal at Newbridge where the chalk arrived by barge from downland quarries to the south. About 150 years ago the pub transferred to the present premises, converted from a row of 16th century workmen's cottages. It has an open L-shaped bar with inglenook fireplaces at each end and a large garden and children's playground at the rear.

The Limeburners is owned by Fuller's Brewery and offers their London Pride, Chiswick Bitter and the stronger HSB. The food menu is varied and includes some unusual dishes such as steak, Stilton and rosti pie as well as curries and a vegetarian selection, for example spinach and red pepper lasagne. The usual snacks (ploughman's lunches, filled baguettes, jacket potatoes and so on) are also on offer. Children and dogs are welcome.

Opening times are 12 noon to 3 pm and 6 pm to 11 pm daily (10.30 pm closing on Sunday evening). Food is served from 12 noon to 2.30 pm and 6.15 pm to 9 pm (9.30 pm on Friday and Saturday). Telephone 01403 782311.

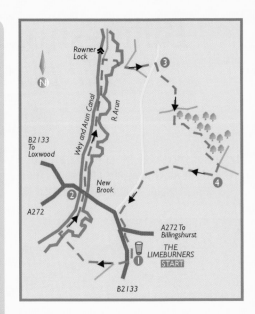

The Walk

① From the pub turn left along the road and, after less than 100 yards, go right along the drive to Guildenhurst Manor until you can fork right over a stile and across a field to the next stile, in sight on the skyline. Go ahead, dropping down to a wide farm bridge over the River Arun, crossing a stile in an intermediate fence en route. Go ahead across a low-lying meadow and turn right to follow the canal with the waterway on your left.

② Cross the A272 and continue along a raised bank with the canal on your left and the river on your right. You will pass the restored Northfield lift-bridge, and, after the best part of a mile, reach the partially restored Rowner Lock. When opposite the lock turn right to walk squarely away from the canal. Cross the river above a sluice and follow a clear track on past the buildings at Rowner Farm and out to a road.

③ Go over the stile opposite and ahead, downhill. Veer slightly left across a field to a second stile. Cross a footbridge and walk round the left edge of the next field, ignoring a signed path off to the left and a gateway ahead. After less than 100 yards, turn squarely right across the middle of the field, go over a metalled drive using two stiles and maintain direction across a

Rowner Lock

meadow to a third stile. Once through a belt of woodland turn left on a narrow path along the edge of the wood. At a junction with another path turn right within a strip of woodland which leads out over a stile into a field corner. Go ahead along a left field edge and, in the next field corner, turn right along the field edge, staying within the same field and ignoring the stile ahead.

④ In the next field corner, with a new recycling centre on your left, turn right, again staying within the same field and following the field edge. In the field beyond, follow the direction of a sign half left, converging on and following the left field edge. If obstructed by a crop, cut

down directly to the left field edge. Whichever route you choose, join the left field edge, follow it out to a lane and turn left. At the A272 bear left and, after taking care for 100 yards beside this busy road, fork right along Lordings Road back to the pub, in sight.

Angmering
The Spotted Cow

MAP: OS EXPLORER 121 (GR 075043) | **WALK 16** | **DISTANCE:** 2¾ MILES

DIRECTIONS TO START: FROM THE A27 AT HAMMERPOT ABOUT 4 MILES EAST OF ARUNDEL FOLLOW THE B2225 SOUTHWARDS. GO LEFT AND RIGHT IN ANGMERING VILLAGE THEN, WHERE THE B2225 BEARS RIGHT, FORK LEFT ALONG A NARROW LANE. THE PUB IS ON THE LEFT AFTER A FEW YARDS. **PARKING:** YOU MAY PARK IN THE PUB CAR PARK WHILE ON THE WALK IF ALSO PATRONISING THE PUB. THERE IS ALSO A LARGE PUBLIC CAR PARK AT THE END OF THE LANE.

The focus of this walk is the National Trust open access area of Highdown Hill, a southern outlier of the Downs overlooking the coastal plain to the west of Worthing. This easy walk takes you gently up to reach the rampart of an Iron Age fort on the summit. Excavations have shown that the area was subsequently occupied by the Romans and that the interior of the fort then became a Saxon burial ground. On a clear day the view along the coast extends from Beachy Head to the Isle of Wight. The return route passes close to Highdown Gardens (see Places of Interest Nearby).

The Spotted Cow

The plain foursquare frontage of this popular dining pub, tucked away along a quiet lane at the edge of the village, is completely transformed during the summer months by a lavish display of hanging baskets, producing a riot of colour. The main feature of the pub is the large dining area, partly housed in a spacious conservatory. It gets very busy, particularly at weekends, so it would be wise to book a table if you are in need of food. Drinkers are, however, well provided for in the comfortable carpeted saloon bar where the tables are unreserved.

The pub is managed on a lease from Scottish and Newcastle and offers a good range of beers, including King and Barnes Sussex, Morland Old Speckled Hen and Courage Directors plus two guest beers. The food menu embraces a wide range of standard fare, all home cooked, as well as daily specials where the emphasis is on fish dishes. Bar snacks such as ploughman's lunches, jacket potatoes, sandwiches and filled baguettes are also available as well as some substantial puddings like banoffi pie or apple crumble and custard.

Opening times are 10.30 am to 3 pm and 5.30 pm to 11 pm on Monday to Friday, 10.30 am to 11 pm on Saturday and 12 noon to 10.30 pm on Sunday. Food is served daily from 12 noon to 2.30 pm and 6.30 pm to 9.30 pm. Telephone: 01903 783979.

The Walk

① From the pub turn left along the lane. A footbridge takes you across a new trunk road. On the other side go ahead along a metalled access drive. Beyond the entrance to a newish house called Ecclesden Paddocks, the drive loses its hard surface.

② After another 100 yards or so, turn left along a narrow fenced path. Where this path ends, turn right through a gap in a fence and go forward along a left field edge, soon on a more substantial track which veers right and left to head, unfenced, across a field, climbing gently but steadily up onto Highdown Hill with expanding views southwards across the coastal plain to the sea and northwards across rolling downland, with the spire of Patching church prominent in the middle distance.

③ Beyond a stile beside a gate you will enter the National Trust public open access area which embraces the summit area of Highdown. Go ahead up to the trig point, from which you get a good view back towards Arundel Castle and the heights of Arundel Park (Walk 13).

④ Walk through the ramparts of the Iron Age fort and on along a clear path. Go through a gap in a ragged hedgerow, to

PLACES OF INTEREST NEARBY

Highdown Gardens, passed on the walk, or accessible by car from the eastbound carriageway of the A259 coast road, are a fine example of a chalk garden, painstakingly created on the site of an old chalk pit, and featuring some rare plant species from the Far East. Admission is free, daily from 10 am to 6 pm during the summer months with more limited winter opening times. Telephone: 01903 239999. Highdown Tea Rooms, nearby, are open from March to October between 9 am and 5 pm.

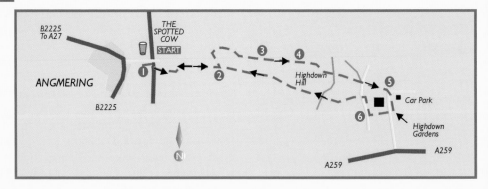

pass close to an iron railed enclosure, leaving the National Trust area but entering another public space, owned and managed by Worthing Borough Council. The rails protect the Miller's Tomb, where John Olliver, a Highdown miller, was buried in 1793. Veer slightly right, dropping gently downhill along a grassy path which brings you to a picnic area and car park.

⑤ Follow the access road from the car park, passing, on your right, the entrances to Highdown Gardens and Highdown Towers, which incorporates a pub, restaurant and teashop. After another 60 yards, fork right along a path which starts to the right of a notice, 'No Horse Riding'. After 30 yards, turn right along the top edge of a mown grassy area. In the field corner, go ahead on a narrow path which takes you to a stile and a junction with a track.

⑥ Turn right, uphill. In the field corner, just short of a gate, turn left and follow a headland path along the top field edge, contouring along the lower hillside and passing through several gates. At a T-junction, turn right. After 20 yards, go left on a hedged bridleway which takes you straight back to point 2. From here you can go ahead, retracing your outgoing route back to the start.

The view from Highdown Hill

Rudgwick
The Kings Head

| **MAP:** OS EXPLORER 134 (GR 090343) | **WALK 17** | **DISTANCE:** $3^3/_4$ MILES |

DIRECTIONS TO START: FROM THE A281 HORSHAM-GUILDFORD ROAD AT BUCKS GREEN, TURN NORTHWARDS ALONG THE B2128 CRANLEIGH ROAD. THE PUB IS ON THE RIGHT AFTER A LITTLE OVER A MILE. **PARKING:** IN THE LARGE PUB CAR PARK WITH PERMISSION.

At first sight Rudgwick is a village without a central focus, spread out beside a long village street. It does, however, have a nucleus of lovely old tile-hung and timber-framed buildings, some with local Horsham stone roofs, mainly clustered near the church and pub. The church has a fine 13th century tower and Norman remnants.

Our walk heads east from the village, traversing the southern slope of the low border ridge between Sussex and Surrey. It is a varied circuit through woods, fields and parkland, mostly on clear, well-trodden paths.

The Kings Head

Most of the Kings Head is housed in an early 18th century cottage, though it is claimed that the northern end incorporates part of a much earlier structure, erected to house the workers employed to build the church which is tucked snugly behind the pub. The premises consist of a bar at one end, warmed by a large wood burning stove on cold days, and a dining area at the other. It is an Enterprise Inn, run on a lease, but serves real ales from a variety of sources, for example Sussex Ale from Harveys of Lewes and Fuller's London Pride. Food at lunchtime includes a 2-course set menu embracing dishes such as escalope of pork or bacon and mushroom pancakes, all prepared and cooked on the premises, as well as filled baguettes. The pub prides itself on its excellent value Sunday roasts and in the evening you can diversify into an extensive menu of Italian specialities.

Opening times are from 11 am to 11 pm on Monday to Saturday and 12 noon to 10.30 pm on Sunday. Food is served from 12 noon to 2 pm on weekdays and 12 noon to 3 pm on Sundays. Children are welcome as are dogs (in the bar only). Telephone: 01403 822200.

The Walk

① From the pub turn left along the main street. Just past Rudgwick chapel on your right turn left along a path which starts to the right and parallel to a driveway. Follow this enclosed path as it meanders down

PLACES OF INTEREST NEARBY

At Howick Farm, about a mile south of Bucks Green, you can visit the **Toyhorse International Stud Farm** with its 600 animals, including a Guinness Record holding toyhorse, only 27" tall. It is open daily from Easter to November. Telephone: 01403 822639.

into a valley. At the bottom go over a footbridge and, where you have a choice of signed paths, keep left, climbing within a wooded strip. Emerge into a field corner and go ahead, walking parallel to the left field edge to a stile, then over a crossing path, forward on another enclosed tree-lined path to a gate and on within the right edge of woodland, ignoring a signed path back to the left.

② Shortly, at a second signed path junction, turn right over a stile and along a left field edge, then left over a second stile and forward, skirting to the right of an equestrian exercise area. With the large house and garden at Hyes in front of you, turn right beside a post and rail fence. Shortly bear left over a stile and forward beside a drive. At a junction of drives go ahead over a stile hidden behind planted trees, through a kissing gate and on beside a hedge to enter woodland.

③ Follow the wide woodland track, ahead, passing several fishing lakes. Cross a footbridge and climb to pass through a bridlegate and on beside a left-hand fence.

④ Join a drive, bear right for 10 yards and then turn left through a gate with a Fire Notice on it and along a gravel track. Keep to the main track through Roman Woods, until a signpost directs you along a track to

Rudgwick church

the right. After a few yards fork left along a narrower grassy path, currently unsigned. Follow more signs to a T-junction where you should turn left along a signed bridleway which crosses a forestry road, descends to a stream crossing and climbs.

⑤ Leave the wood through a gate and head out across a field on an unfenced track, then ahead on a concrete access track. Just past a pair of cottages called Hookwood on the right, fork left along a track, labelled 'No Bridle Way'. Where the track bends left, you have a choice of two parallel paths ahead. Yours is the one on the left, passing through mature beech and oak woodland, then across a field, over a drive and forward on an enclosed path. Join a drive from a cottage and, after 60 yards, go right through an iron kissing gate, across rough pasture and out through Rudgwick churchyard to the road by the Kings Head.

West Chiltington
The Elephant & Castle

DIRECTIONS TO START: WEST CHILTINGTON IS SIGNPOSTED FROM STORRINGTON ON THE A283 ROAD WEST OF ITS JUNCTION WITH THE A24. FROM STORRINGTON FOLLOW THE B2139 AT FIRST, CONTINUING ALONG MINOR ROADS AND LANES. IN WEST CHILTINGTON VILLAGE, TURN RIGHT ALONG CHURCH STREET. THE PUB IS A SHORT DISTANCE PAST THE CHURCH. **PARKING:** PATRONS ARE WELCOME TO USE THE PUB CAR PARK WITH PRIOR PERMISSION.

Although within a mile or so of a large, though pleasantly leafy housing estate to the south, the older village of West Chiltington retains its separate identity and seclusion, being quite difficult to get at by road with a final approach from the south along a narrow deeply sunken lane. The church of Norman origins has an attractive shingled spire. Inside are 12th to 13th century fresco fragments and an unusual tunnel-like leper's squint. Nearby are the old village stocks and whipping post.

Our walk heads north and west towards the village of Nutbourne, using ancient tracks and field paths and passing near Nutbourne Vineyard which incorporates a visitor centre in an old windmill.

The Elephant & Castle

The Elephant & Castle calls itself 'The Village Local' and it is just that, situated in the centre of the old village within yards of the church. The building dates from 1665 and for many years was occupied by officials of the church and parish. It became a beer house in 1830, soon under its present name which refers to the Cutlers' Company, the castle being their trademark and the elephant a symbol of their involvement in the ivory trade. The interior is laid out in traditional style with saloon and public bars on either side of a central serving area.

This is a Hall and Woodhouse pub serving Badger beers – First Gold and Sussex Bitter and a rotating guest beer. A new food menu is under development and will include dishes using meat from beef cattle raised at a local farm, as well as the usual range of traditional pub food and bar snacks. Children are welcome as are dogs.

Opening times are from 11 am to 3 pm and 5 pm to 11 pm on Monday to Thursday, staying open during the afternoon on Friday to Sunday. Food is served from 12 noon to 2.30 pm and 7 pm to 9.30 pm daily. Telephone: 01798 813307.

The Walk

① From the pub, walk back past the church into the village. At a crossroads next to the village shop turn left. After 150 yards where the lane begins to bear left, turn right along a metalled drive. Where the drive ends, go ahead to enter a deeply sunken hollow way, shortly following it round to the left. Where the enclosed path ends abruptly, go ahead across a golf course.

② At a three-armed fingerpost turn right along a tree-lined grassy strip between two golf playing areas. At another sign turn left, dropping down along the right edge of a field with a fine panoramic view southwards to the Downs. At the bottom of the slope turn right along a grassy headland path. At another fingerpost bear left through a bridle gate and along a narrow overgrown path which soon enters another hollow way. At a T-junction with a roughly metalled drive turn right.

③ At Nyetimber Farm go forward past a large weatherboarded barn and, after a few yards, go left, still on a metalled drive. After a little over 100 yards fork left on a grassy path along the right edge of a vineyard until you can go right down steps to join a lane. Go straight ahead through the gateway to Random Cottage. It looks very private but is a public footpath. Go ahead beside a lawn to a bridle gate and on along an enclosed path.

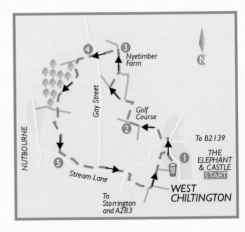

Nyetimber Vineyard

④ Where the path divides, keep left, along the top edge of woodland at first, then obliquely down through the wood. On reaching a drive in front of a cottage, go forward for 10 yards then right along a narrow concrete path which starts down steps, squeezes to the right of a house and garden and comes out in the corner of a field where you should turn left along the left field edge, heading towards the Downs. Continue along the right edge of the next field out to join a lane.

⑤ Turn left and follow the aptly named Stream Lane, accompanied for most of the way by a tiny stream which threatens to erode the tarmac in places. Ignore the first lane off to the left (Gay Street). At a second junction, with a wider road, turn right and immediately left along a tarmac drive, soon passing a fine old converted windmill which still retains two of its sails. Beyond the mill the drive dwindles to a path. At a crossing track turn left. After 10 yards go left on a fenced path along the right edge of two fields. About halfway along the second field ignore a stiled path to the right. In the field corner go forward through a gate. Just short of a second gate go right alongside West Chiltington churchyard wall until you can go through a kissing gate and out past the church to the road. Turn right, back to the start.

> ### PLACES OF INTEREST NEARBY
> West of Nutbourne and signed from the A283, the **Pulborough Brooks RSPB Nature Reserve** incorporates a nature trail with bird hides as well as a visitor centre, shop and tearooms (see Walk 14). Further to the south **Parham Park** is a fine Elizabethan mansion with a spectacular long gallery. The house and gardens are open from April to October on Wednesdays, Thursdays, Sundays and bank holidays (house from 2 pm to 6 pm, gardens from 12 noon to 6 pm).

Dragons Green
The George & Dragon

DIRECTIONS TO START: DRAGONS GREEN IS LESS THAN ½ MILE TO THE NORTH OF THE A272. THE PUB IS SIGNPOSTED FROM THE A272 ABOUT 2 MILES WEST OF THE A272/A24 JUNCTION. **PARKING:** IN THE PUB CAR PARK WITH PRIOR PERMISSION.

It was left to an enthusiastic Dutchman, Pieter Boogaart, in his recent best selling book *Ode to a Road*, to extol the virtues of the countryside on either side of the A272 trunk route which takes an east-west route across the middle of Sussex. This walk leads you through an area of small scale woods and fields within a mile or so of this busy road, heading south from Dragons Green to visit the small village of Shipley with its fine restored windmill and Hilaire Belloc connections. The route uses parts of two of the many north-south droveways which were once used to transport cattle between summer and winter pastures. One of these, locally known as Green Street, has almost fallen out of use, even by walkers, so you can feel like an explorer! South of Shipley we cross a delectable grassy area, now open for public access under the Countryside Stewardship scheme, where the infant River Adur winds through meadows, overlooked by the 12th century church and Shipley Windmill (see Places of Interest Nearby).

The George & Dragon

Originating as a row of 16th century cottages, the George & Dragon, in business since the 19th century, has many of the ideal features of a country pub, including a cosy low-beamed bar and dining area and a fine inglenook fireplace. In the front garden stands, somewhat incongruously, a stone memorial cross, erected in 1893 following the suicidal death by drowning of Walter, the albino son of Alfred and Charlotte Budd, then owners of the pub. The cross stood, at first, in Shipley churchyard but was removed on the orders of the vicar because of the implied criticism in the original inscription which, touchingly, read 'May God forgive those who forgot their duty to him who was just and afflicted.'

The George & Dragon is now a Hall and Woodhouse pub, serving their Badger First Gold and King and Barnes Sussex Bitter. The food menu embraces traditional pub grub such as steak and kidney pie, as well as specials like home-made cheesy topped cottage pie or bacon and onion suet pudding, all prepared and baked on the premises.

Opening times are 12 noon to 3 pm and 6 pm to 11 pm on Monday to Friday, 12 noon to 11 pm on Saturday, 12 noon to 10.30 pm on Sunday. Food is served from 12 noon to 2 pm (3 pm on Sunday) and from 6.30 pm to 9 pm. Children are welcome as are dogs (in the bar area). Telephone: 01403 741320.

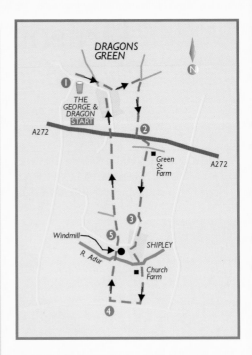

The Walk

① From the pub turn right and, after a few yards, go right again along Bakers Lane. At another road junction go straight ahead and, after less than 100 yards, where the lane bends right, fork left along a short enclosed track to a bridle gate and on along a left field edge. At the field corner go through a gap and turn right to head south along a gravel track. Follow it past two ugly mobile phone masts (why on earth couldn't the two companies involved be required to share the same mast?) and out to the A272.

② Cross the road with care, go over a stile beside a gate, opposite, and continue slightly left across a neglected meadow. Go over a second stile beside a gate, then left along a wide strip which, after 100 yards or so, narrows to a track. After a few more yards, go sharply back to the right

The fine windmill at Shipley

along the unmade access track to a cottage. Go ahead between the cottage on your left and a brick shed on your right to enter an enclosed path, part of the ancient 'Green Street', which may be overgrown. Where the main path curves to the right, go forward through a gap, along a right field edge and on within the right edge of a plantation of conifers. At the far end of the wood go forward along a right field edge out to join a lane.

③ Go ahead along the lane into Shipley. Where the lane bends round to the right go forward along a 'No Through Road' and where it ends, enter Shipley churchyard. On reaching the church porch turn right down steps and leave the churchyard through an iron kissing gate. Go forward for a few yards, and then bear half left across a watermeadow with one of the headwater streams of the River Adur on your right. Cross a substantial footbridge, walk up over a lawn, on past farm buildings and along the farm access drive out to a lane. Turn right.

④ After 300 yards turn right again along a lovely tree-lined track, another section of ancient 'green lane'. Follow it for over $\frac{1}{4}$ mile, back across the river and out via the access drive from Shipley Windmill to join a lane.

⑤ Turn right, and after a few yards, go left over a stile and forward along the right edge of two fields and half left across a third field to go over a stile and culvert to join a track. Turn right to follow this track northwards along the right edge of several fields out to the A272. Cross the road and follow Dragons Lane, opposite, rejoining your outgoing route on a left hand bend and following it back to the start.

PLACES OF INTEREST NEARBY

Shipley Windmill, passed on the walk, is open from 2 pm to 5 pm on the first, second and third Sundays during the summer months. The mill, a fine octagonal white painted smock mill, the largest in Sussex and also one of the most recently built (1879), was restored to working order in 1958 in memory of Hilaire Belloc who lived nearby from 1906 to 1953.

Ashurst
The Fountain Inn

MAP: OS EXPLORER 122 (GR 180161)   **WALK 20**   **DISTANCE:** 3 MILES

DIRECTIONS TO START: ASHURST IS ON THE B2135 WHICH HEADS NORTH FROM THE A283, THE STEYNING BYPASS. THE FOUNTAIN IS BESIDE THE B ROAD AFTER ABOUT 3 MILES. **PARKING:** YOU MAY PARK IN THE PUB CAR PARK WITH PERMISSION.

Ashurst is a village without central focus on the western side of the valley of the River Adur. It is a small scattered settlement consisting of several farms and farmhouses and a handful of residences spread out across a thinly populated agricultural landscape. To begin with we head to the river for a ¾ mile stroll downstream along the raised flood bank to Bineham Bridge. Continuing across low-lying meadows the walk then diverts to the west of the B road to come within easy reach of Ashurst church, an attractive 12th-13th century building, notable as the final resting place of Lord Olivier, the actor, who lived nearby. Church and pub are linked by a short direct field path.

The Fountain Inn

This is a delightful old pub embraced on three sides by spacious gardens and a brick patio at the front. Nearby is a skittle alley with a decked terrace overlooking a small pond. The cosy front bar has a flagstone floor and a large inglenook fireplace. There is another bar at the back and a separate dining area. The writer Hilaire Belloc paused here during his walk across Sussex and observed that 'the Fountain of Ashurst runs, by God's good grace, with better stuff than water' and the beer still flows, currently Harveys Sussex, Fuller's London Pride and a guest beer straight from the barrel. The food, all home prepared and cooked, is of the highest quality. The lunch menu, probably of most interest to walkers, includes several pub favourites like steak, mushroom and ale pie, plus some less familiar fare such as Sussex Smokie – smoked haddock and prawns in a cheese sauce.

Opening times are 11.30 am to 11 pm on Monday to Saturday, 12 noon to 10.30 pm on Sunday. Food is served from 11.30 am to 2.30 pm and 6 pm to 9.30 pm on weekdays and from 12 noon to 3 pm and 6 pm to 8.30 pm on Sunday. Dogs are welcome in the bar but children under 14 are not allowed in the pub. Telephone: 01403 710219.

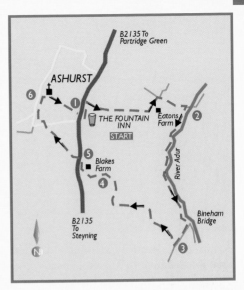

The Walk

① From the pub turn right beside the B2135. After 100 yards, just past the village hall, turn right along the concrete drive to Eatons Farm. On reaching a grassy area just short of the farm, fork left down to a stile beside a gate and go ahead keeping close to the hedge on your right. Ignore the first stile on your right which provides private access to a garden. After another 60 yards go ahead over a second stile, cross a field to another stile and continue to reach the Adur riverbank at Eatons Bridge.

② Don't cross the bridge. Instead, turn right and follow the nearside riverbank downstream, with a distant view of the Downs ahead, for about ³/₄ mile to Bineham Bridge, the next river crossing. Don't cross this bridge either. Instead, go through a gate beside the bridge, continuing forward for a few yards. Just short of a second gate, fork right along a shady tree-lined track.

③ After about 200 yards join and go forward along the drive from a house and, after 30 more yards, turn right over a stile and follow the direction of a fingerpost, heading slightly right across a low-lying meadow. As you approach a

The River Adur

fence and a reed-filled ditch, bear left, walking parallel to this fence and soon heading for a farm gate. Bear right over a stile beside this gate and climb gently along a left field edge. At the top of the slope go over another stile beside a gate and half left along the left edge of the next field. In the field corner turn right, staying within the same field and following the left edge.

④ At the end of the field veer half left through a gate and go forward with a high hedge on your left. The headland path becomes a wide enclosed strip between hedge and ditch. Beyond a gate continue beside the hedge, left, to Blakes Farm where you can walk out through a

PLACES OF INTEREST NEARBY

The adjacent villages of **Steyning** and **Bramber** a few miles to the south are both worth a visit. Steyning has a wealth of old buildings, many timber-framed, and Bramber boasts an atmospheric ruined castle as well as **St Mary's House**, a lovely old medieval timber-framed house, still lived in, but open from Easter to the end of September on Sundays and Thursdays from 2 pm to 6 pm (telephone: 01903 816205).

concrete courtyard to join the B2135 road and turn right.

⑤ After 100 yards or so beside this busy road go left over a stile, forward across two small fields with a plank bridge and stile between them and on over two more stiles. Now head half right gently up across a field with, over to your right, a rather grand red brick house commanding, as you do from this point, a fine view southwards to the Downs. In the top field corner cross a stile into the Ashurst village recreation ground. Exit from the far right corner of this area onto a lane and turn left. Walk past the village school, following the lane round to a road junction where you should go ahead, signposted to the parish church.

⑥ After about 200 yards, the return route to the pub starts along an enclosed path to the right, a few yards short of the church, worth the short there-and-back-detour if time permits. The narrow path from point 6 squeezes along the left edge of several paddocks and continues along the left edge of a field to reach the B2135 opposite the pub.

Maplehurst
The White Horse

MAP: OS EXPLORER 134 (GR 189245)   **WALK 21**   **DISTANCE:** 4 MILES

DIRECTIONS TO START: FROM THE A272 ABOUT 2$\frac{1}{2}$ MILES WEST OF COWFOLD, HEAD NORTH ALONG A LANE, SIGNPOSTED TO MAPLEHURST. AFTER ANOTHER 2 MILES, AT A CROSSROADS IN THE VILLAGE, TURN RIGHT. THE PUB IS ON THE RIGHT AFTER A FEW YARDS. TO APPROACH FROM THE NORTH, TURN OFF THE A281 SOUTH OF MANNINGS HEATH (THEN LEFT AT THE CROSSROADS IN MAPLEHURST).
PARKING: YOU ARE WELCOME TO PARK IN THE PUB CAR PARK (WITH PERMISSION).

This stroll passes through a prosperous countryside dotted with stud farms, large farmhouses and small-scale agricultural holdings. It is a landscape on a modest scale with a generous network of public paths crossing a patchwork of small fields and passing through areas of woodland. Our circuit heads southwards on an undulating route across two valleys cut by streams forming the headwaters of the River Adur. It then encircles Maplehurst to the north with opportunities for short cuts along lanes back to the pub at several points.

The White Horse

Purpose-built as an inn in 1820, the White Horse was extended at the turn of the last century. In recent years the interior has been refurbished with skill and sensitivity, retaining the traditional atmosphere in both the newer part of the pub and the older public bar which still has a stone floor and inglenook fireplace. A conservatory opens onto a large garden with a pleasant view across the valley to the south.

The pub is a free house, offering particularly interesting beers. There are usually three or four locally brewed guest beers on the go, such as Weltons of Horsham, and W J King (late of King and Barnes). The excellent 'pub grub' is all prepared and cooked on the premises and the snacks embrace ploughman's, jackets and sandwiches. Children and dogs are welcome as long as they can get on with the two pub cats, Smudge and Pickles.

Opening times are from 12 noon to 2.30 pm on Monday to Friday, 11.30 am to 2.30 pm on Saturday, and 6 pm to 11 pm on Monday to Saturday; 12 noon to 3 pm and 7 pm to 11 pm on Sunday. Food is served from 12 noon to 2 pm and 7 pm to 9 pm daily. No food on Monday except Bank Holidays. Telephone: 01403 891208.

The Walk

① From the pub turn right along the lane and, after about 300 yards, go right again along the drive to Heathtolt Farm. Walk between the farm buildings and ahead along a grassy path to enter woodland. Go

half left up through the wood. Leave the wood, turn left along the wood edge and, after about 100 yards, squarely right across a field, passing under power lines. Enter woodland over a stile and follow a narrow path downhill.

② At the bottom, leave the wood and turn right, walking parallel to the wood edge on your right through a long thin meadow to join a road over a stile. Turn right. After 350 yards go left along the roughly metalled drive to Joles Farm. Walk past the buildings and on along a rough track with a deer compound on your right. Where this track opens out into a field,

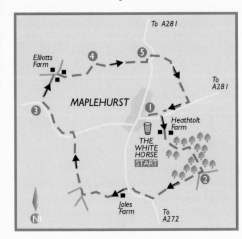

On the walk

turn sharp right through a gate and follow a narrow path with a high deer fence on your right. Where the deer fence veers right, fork left through trees, soon rejoining the fence and dropping down into a dip and across a stream. Shortly bear left across a concrete culvert and right, resuming your previous direction through an area of rough pasture, walking roughly parallel to trees on your right. At the end of this long thin meadow join a road over a stile and turn left.

③ After a little over ¼ mile fork right along a bridleway between hedge and fence which starts between two driveways, the one to the left being to a house called Elliotts. The path emerges onto a drive where you should turn left and, after 40 yards, right between stables and ahead along a wide grassy strip between paddocks. After crossing a gallop, go ahead on a narrower path within a wood edge.

Cross a wide concrete bridge and go forward along a left field edge.

④ In the field corner go ahead through a bridle gate and turn right, climbing gently, walking parallel to a right field edge and skirting to the left of a small pond. Go over a stile a few yards to the left of the next field corner and walk round the right edge of the next field until, after about 100 yards, you can go right over two stiles and on along a left field edge to join a lane. Turn left.

⑤ After about 100 yards, opposite a bungalow called Roberts Lea on the left, turn right through a gate, go ahead to a stile and on along the left edge of a paddock to enter woodland. Follow a clear path through the wood, leave it over a stile and go forward along a track between fence and hedge, following it right and left out to a lane. Turn right, back to Maplehurst.

Lambs Green
The Lamb Inn

MAP: OS EXPLORER 134 (GR 219368)　　　**WALK 22**　　　**DISTANCE:** 2½ MILES

DIRECTIONS TO START: EASIEST ACCESS IS FROM A ROUNDABOUT ON THE A264 CRAWLEY-HORSHAM ROAD AT FAYGATE. HEAD NORTH ALONG A LANE AND TAKE THE FIRST TURNING ON THE RIGHT AFTER 1½ MILES, SIGNPOSTED TO LAMBS GREEN. **PARKING:** IN THE PUB CAR PARK WITH PERMISSION.

Although sandwiched by Crawley to the east and Horsham to the south, the tiny settlement of Lambs Green lies at the centre of a gentle farmed landscape, so far untouched by modern development though how long this will remain so is uncertain if and when Crawley is allowed to spread westwards. The walk explores an inviting patchwork of small fields and woods forming the first impression of the English landscape seen by an arriving traveller from the aircraft window during the final approach to Gatwick Airport from the west. The walk, which links Lambs Green with the more substantial village of Rusper, is an easy one across gently undulating ground, mainly on field paths.

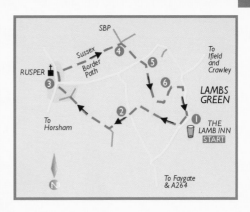

The Lamb Inn

The Lamb Inn has been recorded as a hostelry since 1774 though the present building dates from the mid 19th century. It has many of the familiar attributes of the unspoilt country pub – a large open bar area with flagstone floor and exposed timbers, cosy dining and drinking areas at either end of the main bar and an open fire in winter. There is also a large conservatory to cope with extra diners.

It is a free house serving beers from the local A.J. King's Brewery in Horsham. The food, home cooked, includes many pub favourites as well as less familiar fare such as fresh sardines with garlic butter as a starter and rack of lamb as a main course. Ploughman's lunches are also available and there is a good range of puddings. Children are welcome and the pub is distinctly animal-friendly, welcoming dogs (on leads).

Opening hours are from 11.30 am to 3 pm and 5 pm to 11 pm on Monday to Friday, 11.30 am to 3 pm and 5 pm to 11 pm on Saturday and 12 noon to 4 pm and 7 pm to 10.30 pm on Sunday. Food is served daily from 12 noon to 2 pm and 7 pm to 9.30 pm. Telephone: 01293 871336.

The Walk

① From the pub turn left along the road. After a little over 100 yards, turn right over a stile set back from the road a few yards along a gravel drive. Head out diagonally across the middle of a large field to find a substantial footbridge in the far field corner. Go ahead along a right field edge, walking round two sides of this field. In the second field corner go over a stile and along a short enclosed path out to a road.

② Go left for 10 yards only, then right over a stile hidden in the hedge. Follow a left field edge, passing a large house on your left. In the field corner go over two stiles in quick succession and maintain direction along the left edge of the field beyond. In the next field corner, ignoring a stile on your left, go forward through a gateway and ahead on a well-trodden path across a field and then along a grassy strip between fences. Cross a stable yard, go ahead over a stile and follow a narrow enclosed path past gardens. At a car park bear left between posts and out to the road at Rusper.

③ Turn right past the Star Inn on your right. At a road junction keep left along the village street. Just short of the church on your left, turn right along a metalled drive to the right of a car dealer's forecourt, signposted as the Sussex Border Path. Where the drive ends go ahead across parkland where there is a well-trodden path. From the far left corner of this area a short enclosed path

Rusper church

leads to a swing gate leading out into a field corner. Go forward along a left field edge for a few yards, through a gap in a hedge and on in the same direction, unfenced between two fields.

④ Walk through a narrow belt of trees and, at a sign where the Sussex Border Path goes off to the left, you should turn right along a field edge with the trees on your right. Go across a culvert in a dip and forward along the right edge of the field beyond to join a road.

⑤ The next path starts over a stile, almost opposite, and follows the right edge of a meadow to a stile, from which a path continues within a wooded strip along the right edge of another large field. After leaving the trees go ahead along a right field edge. In the corner go through a gap and turn left along the left

edge of a small field following a line of oak trees on your left.

⑥ In the field corner side step to the left through a gap and resume your previous direction, now with a stream on your right. Shortly go forward along a more substantial track until you can go right through a gap in a post and rail fence and along a short enclosed path which skirts to the left of a garden and comes out on a lane. Turn right, back to the start.

PLACES OF INTEREST NEARBY

Gatwick Zoo, to the north at Charlwood, is a small family-run establishment set in 10 acres with a variety of birds and small mammals on display, plus two tropical houses. It is open from 10.30 am to 6 pm between March and October, 10.30 am to 4 pm from November to February (closed Christmas and Boxing Days). Telephone: 01293 862313.

Colgate
The Dragon

| MAP: OS EXPLORER 134 (GR 229328) | **WALK 23** | DISTANCE: $2^1/_4$ OR $4^1/_4$ MILES |

DIRECTIONS TO START: COLGATE IS ON THE UNCLASSIFIED ROAD LINKING PEASE POTTAGE WITH HORSHAM AND CAN BE REACHED EITHER FROM THE A264 HORSHAM-CRAWLEY ROAD AT FAYGATE OR FROM THE A23 BRIGHTON-LONDON ROAD AT PEASE POTTAGE. **PARKING:** IN THE LARGE PUB CAR PARK WITH PERMISSION.

Although nominally covering 8,000 acres at the western end of the High Weald Area of Outstanding Natural Beauty, St Leonard's Forest has been reduced by earlier clearance to a patchwork of woods and fields. It is still a most attractive and well-wooded landscape characterised by alternating ridges and valleys carved by modest streams or gills draining southwards to form the River Arun.

Our walk, offering longer and shorter options, starts high on one of the forest ridges and follows an up and down route to cross and re-cross two of these tiny gills, passing through alternate field and woodland.

The Dragon

Occupying relatively modern premises, the Dragon is laid out in traditional pub style with a comfortable carpeted saloon at one end and a more spartan public bar at the other. At the back is a spacious garden surrounded by trees. It is a Hall and Woodhouse pub, run on a tenancy, serving Badger First Gold plus King and Barnes Best Bitter, now a Badger beer following the absorption of the distinguished King and Barnes Horsham Brewery into the Hall and Woodhouse empire.

An extensive traditional pub menu is available, as well as a good choice of filled jacket potatoes and 'speciality' sandwiches, with interesting fillings such as chicken, bacon and brie or Mediterranean bruschetta.

Opening hours are 11 am to 3 pm and 5 pm to 12 midnight on Monday to Thursday, 11.30 am to 3.30 pm and 4.30 pm to 1 am on Friday, 11 am to 1 am on Saturday and 12 noon to 12 midnight on Sunday. Telephone: 01293 851206.

The Walk

① Start the walk along Springfield Lane, which leaves the Pease Pottage-to-Horsham road beside the pub. Follow it for $^1/_2$ mile until, about 100 yards beyond the point where it dwindles to a gravel access drive, you can fork left over two stiles in quick succession and continue along a right field edge. Cross two more stiles and, ignoring a left fork, go directly ahead, dropping down within the right hand edge of woodland. Beyond the wood, continue on a narrow fenced path between two fields, on across a stream (Pyefall Gill) in a wooded dip and sharply up within the left edge of more woodland. At a T-junction with a wider track, turn left and follow it out via an access drive to join a lane. (For the shorter $2^1/_4$ mile walk turn left along the lane, rejoining the longer walk at point 4.)

② For the longer walk cross the road and go ahead along a wide tree-lined track. Beyond a stile built into a gate go ahead with a fence, left, to join another road and turn left. After about 300 yards, turn right along a narrow signed path which drops down along the left edge of a paddock, squeezed between fences at first, then down through an area of heath and open woodland. Cross a stream (Newstead Gill), leave the wood and climb along a left field edge to join a metalled farm road.

③ Turn left between the buildings of Newstead Farm. The hard road becomes a

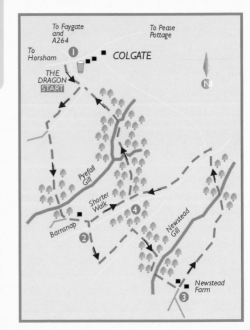

The path down towards Newstead Gill

dirt track and contours along the upper slope of the valley with good views to your left. Beyond a gate, follow the direction of a fingerpost half left, obliquely down a grassy slope to re-enter woodland through a bridle gate. Follow a clear path back over Newstead Gill and up through the wood to join a road and turn left. At a road junction fork right along Woodlands Lane.

④ After another 350 yards, where the shorter walk rejoins, turn right along a path within the right edge of woodland. After only a few yards, go right over a stile and head half left across rough pasture where there is a faint trodden path, then down through woodland. Re-cross Pyefall

> **PLACES OF INTEREST NEARBY**
>
> **Leonardslee Gardens,** a few miles to the south on the A281, are notable for a spectacular display of rhododendrons and azaleas in the spring. Wallabies live semi-wild in the wooded valley and there is a restaurant, shop and bonsai exhibition. The gardens are open daily from March to October, 9 am to 5 pm. Telephone: 01403 891212.

Gill and continue through the wood, bearing round to the right between fences then left on a causeway, passing two small ponds. A path climbs steeply ahead to reach a T-junction. Turn left out to Springfield Lane and right, retracing your outgoing route, back to the pub.

Bolney
The Eight Bells

DIRECTIONS TO START: BOLNEY VILLAGE IS SIGNPOSTED NORTHWARDS FROM THE A272 ROAD SOME YARDS WEST OF ITS JUNCTION WITH THE A23. THE PUB IS ON THE LEFT AFTER A FEW YARDS. **PARKING:** YOU MAY PARK IN THE PUB CAR PARK WITH PERMISSION. SOME ALTERNATIVE ROADSIDE PARKING IS POSSIBLE FURTHER NORTH ALONG THE VILLAGE STREET.

Although close to the busy intersection of two trunk roads, this is a tranquil walk through a completely unspoilt area of parkland, fields and small patches of woodland, mostly on clear paths with few hills. The walk starts at the original nucleus of the village of Bolney, clustered round the pub and the church, of Norman origins, with a tower dating from 1538. After skirting to the east of the village, we head north to enter Wykehurst Park, with a good view of Wykehurst Place, a turreted French-chateau style mansion built in 1872. The route continues through small woods and along a sunken track, probably of ancient origin.

The Eight Bells

An inn of some kind has occupied the site of the Eight Bells for about 400 years. The present pub, which probably derives its name from the full peal of bells in the nearby parish church, is still an unpretentious village 'local', incorporating an unimproved public bar with brick floor and open fire, a smaller lounge bar and a cosy dining area. Outside, the spacious garden has a terraced lawn with tables and benches and a small lily pond. Notable on the good traditional pub menu are home made pot meals such as cottage pie, macaroni cheese and beef stew or, for a snack, you can choose from filled baguettes, jacket potatoes or ploughman's lunches. The beer on draught is Harveys Sussex Bitter.

Opening times are 11 am to 11 pm on Monday to Thursday (12 midnight on Friday and Saturday) and 12 noon to 11 pm on Sunday. Food is served from 12 noon to 3 pm and from 6 pm to 9 pm except Sunday and Monday evenings. Children and dogs are equally welcome. Telephone: 01444 881396.

The Walk

① Start the walk up steps and through a rather grand lychgate into the churchyard opposite the pub. Skirt to the left of the church, leave the churchyard and go ahead, passing the village school on your left. Go forward on a path, enclosed at first, then along a left field edge, out to a lane.

② Turn left and, after 60 yards, go right through a gate to follow a well-trodden

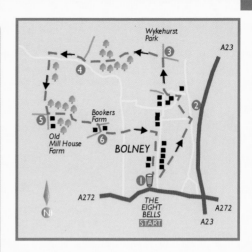

path through an area of pasture and scrub to join another lane. Turn right and, at a road junction, left. Where the lane curves left, go right along a drive, signposted as part of the High Weald Landscape Trail. Where this drive, in turn, bears left, go ahead through a gateway and along an enclosed path which climbs gently, northwards.

③ About 80 yards after passing beneath a stone and brick arched bridge turn left through the remains of a kissing gate and forward along a fenced path across parkland with a good view to the right across the valley to Wykehurst Place. Where the enclosed path ends at a swing gate, go ahead, downhill beside a right-hand fence to find another kissing gate not far from the bottom right field corner. Cross a stream and bear half left across the corner of a field passing two lofty pine trees. Enter woodland through a kissing gate and follow a clear path through this dense coppice. A path continues round the left edge of a garden and then left along the gravel drive from a house out to join a lane.

Wykehurst Park

④ Bear right along the lane and, after a few yards, at a road junction, go straight ahead. After another 300 yards or so, go left over a stile, follow a fence to a second stile and continue along a woodland path which, after a while, becomes a fine hollow way between tree-lined banks.

⑤ Where the path emerges at Old Mill House Farm, double sharply back to the left and, after 10 yards, go right over a stile to follow a fenced path beside a garden. Follow this path as it wobbles left and right to enter dense woodland where it follows a raised causeway beside a swampy area. Beyond a footbridge, where the path divides, turn right. Shortly leave the wood over a stile and turn right to follow a right field edge until you can go right over a stile beside a gate and forward beside two sheds.

⑥ At a junction with an access drive turn left and follow it out between two fields of vines to reach a lane. The path back to Bolney starts over the stile opposite and takes you out to the village street where you can turn right, back to the start.

PLACES OF INTEREST NEARBY

About 5 miles to the north along the A23, at Handcross, is **Nymans Garden**, bequeathed to the National Trust in 1954. It covers 30 acres and contains many rare shrubs and conifers, some from the southern hemisphere. Open from March to early November, daily except Monday and Tuesday, 11 am to 6 pm. Telephone: 01444 400321.

Pyecombe
The Plough

MAP: OS EXPLORER 122 (GR 292124) | **WALK 25** | DISTANCE: 3 MILES

DIRECTIONS TO START: PYECOMBE VILLAGE AND PUB ARE SITUATED TO THE NORTH OF THE A23/A273 JUNCTION, ABOUT 5 MILES OUT OF BRIGHTON, SANDWICHED BETWEEN THE TWO ROADS AND SIGNPOSTED FROM BOTH. **PARKING:** THERE IS AMPLE ROOM TO PARK ALONG THE OLD A23 (NOW A CUL-DE-SAC) NEXT TO THE PUB.

Wolstonbury Hill, at 677 ft, is one of the grandest summits on the South Downs, jutting out from the northern escarpment, and thereby commanding superb views, particularly westwards along the line of the Downs to Chanctonbury Ring and across a valley to another fine downland height, Newtimber Hill. Crowned by the remains of an Iron Age fort, Wolstonbury is now managed by the National Trust who have cleared the hilltop of the scrub which had threatened to engulf much of the area a few years ago.

Our walk offers a steady well-graded climb to the top of the hill and back by a different route. There is plenty of scope for varying or extending the walk within the National Trust open access area, now marked on OS Explorer maps. The lovely little church at Pyecombe, passed near the start of the walk, is notable for a rare 12th century lead font.

The Plough

As its location suggests, the Plough was once a busy coaching inn, offering the first or last change of horses on the main road between London and Brighton. The exterior of the main building remains much as it was, but in recent years the interior has been completely transformed from a basic village local into a smart dining pub. The shiny new wood floor is matched by well-designed modern tables, chairs and bench seats. The main bar area at the front leads into a spacious conservatory dining room which in turn opens out onto a brick patio on two levels at the side and rear of the pub.

The Plough is a free house in private ownership, offering a choice of three beers on hand pump, currently Harveys Sussex Bitter, Morland Old Speckled Hen and Fuller's London Pride. The menu is particularly interesting – international but with a strong Italian accent, including a wide choice of pasta dishes and pizzas. A Sunday lunch roast is also on offer. The snack menu is a sophisticated one, embracing foccacia sandwiches with fillings such as prawn and avocado with chive mayonnaise.

Opening times are from 11 am to 11 pm on Monday to Saturday and 12 noon to 10.30 pm on Sunday. Children are welcome but dogs are not allowed in the pub. Telephone: 01273 842796.

The Walk

① From the front door of the pub turn left and immediately left again along Church Lane. At a crossroads, with Pyecombe church hidden away to your

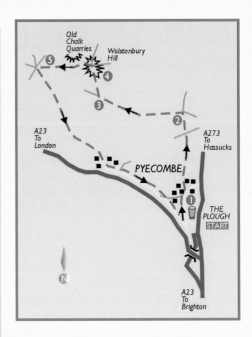

left, go ahead along a lane called The Wyshe which soon narrows to a hedged path and climbs steadily up onto the Downs. Ignore the first signed crossing path.

② At a major junction of tracks turn left on a path which starts through a bridle gate. Climb steadily across glorious open sheep pasture, walking parallel to a fence, away to your left, and eventually joining a track beside this fence. From this rising path you get a good view back to Jack and

PLACES OF INTEREST NEARBY

Clayton Mills can be reached along a lane from the A273 about a mile north of Pyecombe. The tower mill, 'Jack', has been converted into a private residence and is not open to the public. The post mill, 'Jill', has been restored to working order and is open to view on summer Sunday afternoons.

The view north from Wolstonbury Hill

Jill, the twin windmills on Clayton Hill. As the ground levels out go through a bridle gate and on along a fenced track.

③ After another 100 yards, just as the ground begins to fall away ahead, go right through a gap in the fence and along a trodden path up to the top of Wolstonbury Hill. To take in the full view make a complete circuit of the low grassy ramparts before homing in on the summit trig point.

④ From the trig point head westwards on a well-trodden path. Cross the ramparts and continue on a clear path, with the scar of an active chalk quarry in view ahead as a marker confirming that you are following the right line. The path descends along the rim of a disused chalk quarry on your right to a stile and then drops more steeply down across an area of pasture, a good spot for chalk downland wildflowers in the early summer. Cross a ditch and bear left for 30 yards down to join a track at a waypost. Turn right and, after five yards, where the track divides, fork left. The path narrows to burrow through an area of scrub and reach a crossing path at a National Trust notice.

⑤ At this point turn left through a bridle gate and immediately left again. Ignoring a stiled path to the right, follow a track, enclosed by high hedges, along the flank of Wolstonbury Hill. Join and go ahead along a wider unmade farm track which drops down and brings you out via a short lane to the end of a cul-de-sac, part of the former A23. Follow this wide road, walking parallel to the new trunk road, over the hedge on your right, for $\frac{1}{2}$ mile or so, back to the start.

Cuckfield
Ye White Harte Inne

<table>
<tr><td>**MAP:** OS EXPLORER 135 (GR 303246), WITH A TINY SECTION ON 134</td><td>**WALK 26**</td><td>**DISTANCE:** 2¾ MILES</td></tr>
</table>

DIRECTIONS TO START: CUCKFIELD IS AT THE JUNCTION OF THE B2036 AND B2184 ROADS ABOUT 2 MILES WEST OF HAYWARDS HEATH VIA THE A272 WHICH NOW BYPASSES THE VILLAGE. **PARKING:** IN THE VILLAGE CAR PARK, A FEW YARDS ALONG THE ROAD WHICH HEADS EAST FROM THE MINI-ROUNDABOUT HALFWAY UP THE HIGH STREET. IF FULL THERE SHOULD BE ROOM TO PARK BESIDE THE ROAD BEYOND THE CAR PARK ENTRANCE.

Although in a commuter area which is vulnerable to further housing development, Cuckfield has, so far, retained its integrity as an individual community. Although staying close to the built up area as it makes a complete circuit of the village, the walk is surprisingly rural, much of it passing through old parkland. After starting out alongside the rolling acres of Cuckfield Park, from which the public are sadly excluded, the walk passes through a delightful area of woodland, managed as a local nature reserve, before crossing higher ground with fine views southwards to the Downs.

Ye White Harte Inne

In spite of its archaic adopted name, the White Harte has only been a pub since 1881, successor to an alehouse which stood in the present churchyard, though the building dates back to the 15th century. In the late 19th century it was a coaching inn on what was once the main road from London but it is now a good village local, owned by Hall and Woodhouse and run on a tenancy. The premises have a traditional layout, with two bars, both with log fires in winter – a carpeted dining area at one end and a public bar with scrubbed wood floors at the other. Outside there is a small sheltered patio.

The good value pub food menu, supplemented by regularly changed blackboard specials, offers most of the old favourites plus vegetarian options such as Thai food in the evenings. Opening hours are 11.30 am to 2 pm and 6 pm to 11 pm on Monday to Friday (except Monday lunchtime), 11.30 am to 11 pm on Saturday and 12 noon to 10 pm on Sunday. Food is served daily from 12 noon to 2 pm (except Monday lunchtime) and in the evening. Dogs are welcome, as are families in the dining area at lunchtime. Telephone: 01444 413454.

The Walk

① From the car park, return to the main village street and turn left to walk south out of the village passing the White Harte on your way. About 100 yards beyond the pub, on the edge of the village, fork right through a wicket gate and forward with iron park railings on your left, continuing along the left edge of two fields with a

PLACES OF INTEREST NEARBY

Borde Hill Garden, about 2 miles to the north-east of Cuckfield, contains many rare plant species collected by the Stephenson Clarke family, who have lived there since 1893. It is laid out within a series of themed garden areas, all set in 200 acres of parkland. The gardens are open daily from 10 am to 6 pm (or dusk if earlier). Telephone: 01444 412151.

kissing gate between them. Beyond another kissing gate the path drops down along the edge of an area of rough pasture which is now reverting to woodland.

② At the bottom of the hill cross a footbridge in a wooded dip and, after 5 yards, go right through an iron gate into New England Wood, a local nature reserve. (Note that the permissive route through this wood is not marked on the Explorer map.) Follow a clear path through this lovely old wood and, where it divides, keep right. The path dips to

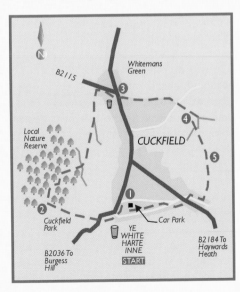

Cuckfield

cross two minor streams. Where the path divides again turn right over a footbridge, and, after 5 yards, turn left with your back to another substantial footbridge, climbing within the right wood edge. Shortly, ignoring a left fork, go forward over a stile and continue uphill along the left edge of three fields. At the top of the third field, side step to the left over a stile and resume your previous direction along an enclosed path which takes you, via an access drive, out to the B2115 at Whitemans Green. Turn right.

③ At a roundabout by the Ship Inn, go straight ahead along a signed public footpath which starts between fences and then skirts to the left of a housing estate, taking you through to another lane. Cross the road and follow the pavement beside Longacre Crescent, opposite. After 10 yards, where the road bends left, go ahead along a gravel drive towards a gate.

④ Just short of this gate, fork right through a smaller gate. You now have a choice of trodden paths. Fork half right on a vaguely defined path which drops obliquely down across an area of rough pasture with views southwards to the Downs. Shortly you can aim for a fingerpost where you can bear right over a stile and drop down with a ragged hedge on your right. After a few yards fork half left across the middle of a field.

⑤ In the far field corner drop down a bank to a stile and bear right on a grassy strip between two gardens at Horsgate Farm and on along an access drive for about $\frac{1}{4}$ mile. On reaching a road at a junction, turn right and follow it round a left hand bend out to a road junction. Go forward for a few yards to a second road junction, turn right and, almost immediately, fork left along Courtmead Road, a private road but also a public footpath. Where this road ends go ahead along a tarmac path to Cuckfield church. From the corner of the church the churchyard exit to the right leads out to the High Street and the exit ahead takes you directly to the back entrance of the White Harte.

Balcombe
The Half Moon

MAP: OS EXPLORER 135 (GR 309307)   **WALK 27**   **DISTANCE:** 3 MILES

DIRECTIONS TO START: BALCOMBE IS ON THE B2036 CUCKFIELD-HORLEY ROAD AND THE PUB IS AT THE CENTRE OF THE VILLAGE TO THE EAST OF THE MAIN ROAD, ACCESSIBLE ALONG TWO ALTERNATIVE LANES TO THE NORTH OF BALCOMBE STATION. **PARKING:** THERE IS LIMITED ROADSIDE PARKING ALONG THE SHORT CUL-DE-SAC BESIDE THE PUB.

Balcombe lies deep in the hilly wooded countryside of the Western High Weald, one of the most beautiful areas of Sussex. The sandstone ridge which is the predominant feature of the district is broken by a series of valleys cut by streams flowing southwards to form the Ouse, interrupted in recent years by the Ardingly Reservoir. Starting on high ground our walk drops down to cross and re-cross one of these delightful valleys, well to the north of the reservoir, following a pleasant mix of field and woodland paths. The return route passes close to Balcombe Lake before climbing steadily back up to the village and the pub. An extension, which would double the length of the walk, is possible from point 4, across the next valley and up to Wakehurst Place (see Places of Interest Nearby).

The Half Moon

Over 300 years old, the Half Moon operated in earlier times as a hostelry for agricultural workers on the Balcombe estate. It also doubled as a centre for the coroner dealing with the multiple fatalities suffered by the railway navvies building the nearby Ouse Viaduct on the London to Brighton railway. More recently, following a period of decline, it has been revitalised under new management and is now very much the centre of life in the village. The large open bar area forms a horseshoe on two levels with a public bar at one end and a comfortable dining section at the other. Outside there is a small walled terrace facing onto the village street, so close to the road that the old style road signpost stands on the patio among the pub tables, indicating the way to London!

The beer on hand pump is Harveys Sussex and at least one other beer and the menu offers an excellent choice of reliable pub fare and locally sourced game specialities. The snack menu includes freshly baked filled baguettes as well as ploughman's lunches and filled jacket potatoes.

Opening times are from 11.30 am to 12 midnight on Monday to Saturday and 12 noon to 12 midnight on Sunday. Food is served from 12.30 pm to 2.30 pm and 6.30 pm to 9 pm daily. Dogs and children are welcome. Telephone: 01444 811582.

The Walk

① Set out along the short cul-de-sac which starts beside the pub, passing the Balcombe village stores on your left. Where the road ends bear right, now on an access drive, signed as a public footpath. After a little over 100 yards go left through an iron kissing gate and ahead along the left edge of parkland with Balcombe House and garden in view across a ha-ha to your left. Shortly go ahead through a kissing gate and drop down through woodland, ignoring a signed path to the right. A wooden causeway takes you across a swampy area and out to a metalled drive where you should turn right.

② After about 600 yards, just beyond a bridge with stone parapet walls, turn right along a path which climbs steadily through more open woodland. Leave the wood and go forward across a field, walking parallel to a line of large trees on your right. After 100 yards, on reaching the corner of a wood, bear half right across a field. Go over a stile beside a gate in the far corner and immediately, at a Y-junction, fork left along a once-metalled track, now reverting to grass.

③ After crossing another stile beside a gate, go left over a plank bridge into Great

> ### PLACES OF INTEREST NEARBY
> Accessible on foot (see above) or, by car, along a circuitous route using narrow lanes to the east of the village is **Wakehurst Place**, managed as a rural outpost of the Royal Botanic Gardens at Kew by the National Trust and containing many rare plant species as well as a spectacular display of azaleas and rhododendrons in the spring. It is open every day except Christmas. Telephone: 01444 894066. Recently established nearby is the lottery funded **National Seed Bank**.

Wood. Follow a clear path through this fine, well-managed area of mature beach and oak interspersed with new planting. Leave the wood over a stile and veer slightly left across a field. Skirt to the right of a house and garden and continue for a few more yards to join a lane. Turn right.

The wooden causeway near the start of the walk

④ After about 350 yards turn right again along the gravel track to Forest Farm. (*The path to Wakehurst starts over a stile on the left a few yards further along the road, returning the same way.*) Where the Forest Farm drive bears away to the right, go ahead over a stile and forward along a left field edge with Balcombe in view ahead across the valley. In the field corner go over a stile beside a gate and veer half left across a field to another stile/gate combination in the far field corner. Turn right along a right field edge and out to join a concrete drive.

⑤ Turn left and follow this drive down into a valley and across a dam at the head of Balcombe Lake. On the other side of the dam go right through a kissing gate, forward, parallel to a fence on your right, to reach a similar stile and then uphill across a field veering very slightly left. At a crossing hedge, turn left, staying within the same field with a hedge on your right. In the field corner go through a kissing gate, forward on a short enclosed path, then round the right edge of a cricket pitch until you can go right through a gap and ahead along the drive from the Cricket Club premises, back to Balcombe.

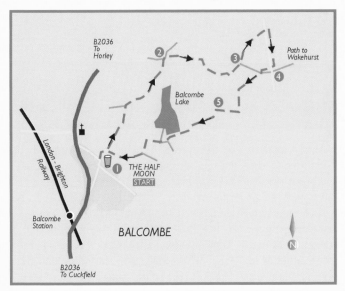

Scaynes Hill
The Farmers

| MAP: OS EXPLORER 135 (GR 368231) | **WALK 28** | DISTANCE: $2\frac{1}{2}$ MILES |

DIRECTIONS TO START: SCAYNES HILL IS ON THE A272 ABOUT 3 MILES EAST OF HAYWARDS HEATH AND THE PUB IS SET BACK TO THE SOUTH OF THE MAIN ROAD IN THE CENTRE OF THE VILLAGE. **PARKING:** IN THE PUB CAR PARK WITH PERMISSION.

Scaynes Hill is a relatively modern village in commuter country to the east of Haywards Heath but we are quickly away into a peaceful Low Wealden landscape. The walk is a short and easy one, following a gently undulating route which starts out along a sunken track and then crosses a patchwork of small fields to enter Great Wood, a good spot for bluebells in the spring. Although as yet untouched by the housing estates spreading out from Haywards Heath, it may not be long before this quietly attractive countryside is threatened by development, unprotected as it is by any special designation like the Areas of Outstanding Natural Beauty in the High Weald, not far to the north, and the Downs to the south. Enjoy it while you can.

The Farmers

Set well back from the main road and insulated from it by a pond and a patch of common land, merging seamlessly with the pub lawn, the Farmers is a spacious road house, part of the Enterprise Inn chain. Until the 1960s it was the Anchor Inn, named after nearby woodland. The old name is retained by the pond in front of the pub, once fed by springs and used to water cattle and the coach horses.

The Farmers offers a warm welcome to walkers and the bill of fare is well geared to their needs. The beer on hand pump is Harveys Sussex Ale. The lunch menu, of most interest to walkers, includes a wide choice of snacks and main courses embracing several vegetarian specials. Children are allowed in the dining room, lounge and back garden and dogs are also welcome.

Opening times are 11 am to 3 pm and 5 pm to 11 pm on Monday to Friday, 11 am to 11 pm on Saturday and 12 noon to 10.30 pm on Sunday. Food is served from 11.30 am to 2.30 pm and 6.30 pm to 9 pm on Monday to Saturday and from 12 noon to 6 pm on Sunday. Telephone: 01444 831419.

The Walk

① To orientate yourself for the start of the walk stand immediately in front of the pub with your back to it. Turn right and follow the right hand access drive from the pub out towards the main road. About 30 yards short of the A272 turn right on a path which skirts to the right of a house and garden, crosses a drive and drops

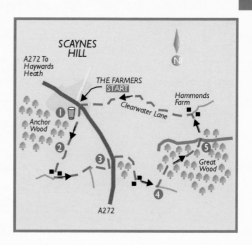

down between wooded banks, damp and uneven in places.

② Where the path finally emerges go ahead along a metalled drive, skirting to the right of a cottage. At a T-junction turn left, still on a drive which you can follow between a fine avenue of horse chestnut trees with views southwards to the Downs, out to the A272. Turn left beside this busy road. Luckily there is a good pavement.

③ After less than 100 yards turn right through a gate and go ahead along a right field edge. Skirt to the left of a clump of mature oak trees, go over a stile and bear half right across a field to a gate. Go forward past a pond on your left, dry at the time of writing, and, at a T-junction with an access track, turn left. Just past a barn on your right go ahead through a gate labelled 'Public Footpath' and forward along a left field edge.

④ In the field corner go right for 30 yards, left over a stile and immediately left again over a second stile. Go forward along a left field edge. In the next field corner cross a

A pond near Hammonds Farm

third stile and, after a few yards, go right over a fourth stile into Great Wood. A few yards into the wood, fork left along a narrow path. After joining a wider track go forward for 20 yards before turning left, downhill, still on a clear track. At the bottom of the slope, turn right along a rutted grass track, walking beside a newly planted area of trees.

⑤ At a junction with another track, go forward over an unobtrusive brick culvert and along a right field edge. At a T-junction with the roughly metalled access track from Hammonds Farm, signposted as the Sussex Border Path, turn left and follow it for a little over ½ mile to the A272 at Scaynes Hill within yards of the pub.

PLACES OF INTEREST NEARBY

Four miles to the east via North Chailey and the A275 are the fine landscaped gardens of **Sheffield Park**, best in the spring when the four lakes are surrounded by a mass display of azaleas and rhododendrons as well as daffodils and bluebells. This National Trust property is open daily (except Mondays) from March to Christmas. Telephone: 01875 790231. Sheffield Park is also the southern terminus of the **Bluebell Railway** (see Places of Interest Nearby – Walk 29).

Horsted Keynes
The Green Man

MAP: OS EXPLORER 135 (GR 385282) | **WALK 29** | **DISTANCE:** $3\frac{1}{4}$ MILES

DIRECTIONS TO START: HORSTED KEYNES IS SIGNPOSTED FROM THE A275 LEWES-FOREST ROW ROAD AT DANEHILL OR, IF APPROACHING FROM THE WEST, FROM THE B2028 NORTH OF LINDFIELD. THE PUB IS IN THE CENTRE OF THE VILLAGE. **PARKING:** THE VILLAGE CAR PARK IS SIGNPOSTED FROM THE ROAD ALMOST OPPOSITE THE PUB OR YOU CAN PARK IN THE PUB CAR PARK WITH PRIOR PERMISSION.

The walk starts by heading north along a quiet lane to the parish church with its Norman tower and soaring shingled spire. In the churchyard, sheltered by a low beech hedge, is the Macmillan family grave, burial place of Harold Macmillan. Inside the church look out for the 13th century effigy of a knight in armour, possibly a member of the Keynes family who gave the village its name. A path leads on through woodland and past a large lake, one of a string of hammer ponds once used to provide a flow of water to power the forges of the iron smelting industry which flourished in the area before 1800. Turning south, we pass the access lane to Horsted Keynes station, making it possible to break off the walk for a steam-hauled trip on the Bluebell Line (see Places of Interest Nearby). The return route is mostly along field paths.

The Green Man

The original Green Man burned down 100 years ago and was replaced by the present pub, nicely situated facing onto the long narrow village green, part of which is incorporated into the pub lawn where you can sit out in summer under brightly coloured umbrellas. Inside, a fragment of the old pub survives in the form of a section of the bar and a large inglenook fireplace. The reconstruction retains a plain wooden floor in the bar which is traditionally decorated with horse brasses. At the other end of the pub is a carpeted dining area.

The Green Man is a Greene King pub selling their own IPA and rotating guest beers. The food menu specialises in local game pies and also features daily specials, regularly rotated. A good selection of vegetarian alternatives is always available.

Opening times are 12 noon to 3 pm and 5.30 pm to 11 pm on Monday to Friday, 12 noon to 11 pm on Saturday and 12 noon to 10.30 pm on Sunday. Food is served daily from 12 noon to 2.30 pm and 6.30 pm to 9 pm (No food on Sunday or Monday evening.) Children over 5 are welcome in the restaurant and dogs on a lead in the bar. Telephone: 01825 790656.

The Walk

① From the pub turn right and, after 60 yards, go right again between low concrete posts. Join and go ahead along Church Lane. Continue on a drive which skirts to the left of the church until, opposite the village school on your right, you can turn left along a dirt track. Follow this track as it skirts to the right of Old Mill House, a fine timber-framed building.

② At a four-armed signpost turn right, still on a clear track which crosses a raised dam at the head of a lake. Shortly fork left with the main track, cross the lake outflow stream and, after another 30 yards, turn left over an elaborate trio of plank bridges and follow a winding path up through woodland, ignoring a crossing path. Leave the wood over a stile and go ahead within a strip of pasture, on to join a road and turn left. A turning on the right leads to Horsted Keynes station on the Bluebell Railway, about $^{1}/_{4}$ mile away, but the walk continues ahead along the road.

③ Where the road bends left, fork right along a farm access drive. At Great Oddynes Farm, where you have a choice of parallel tracks ahead, keep to the one on the right. Pass between the farm buildings and, beyond the farm, go ahead with a hedge on your left, over a stile beside a gate and on, now with a hedge on your right. Cross a bridge over the Bluebell Railway and follow a right field edge.

④ In the field corner turn left, staying

A former hammer pond passed on the walk

out to a road. Turn left.

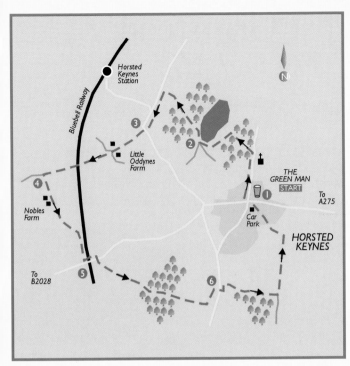

⑥ After 100 yards or so go right to a gate, forward to a second gate, on beside a paddock to a stile and across a field. The path continues through a wood and up to a T-junction with a wide track where you should turn left. Where the track divides, fork right along a gravel drive and then along a grassy path parallel and to the right of the drive. Continue along a left field edge to a stile in the corner, on past a bungalow, then left and right to rejoin the metalled drive. Where the drive curves right, go ahead along an unmade access drive which takes you out to the road within yards of the pub.

within the same field and ignoring the stile ahead. After skirting to the left of a cottage at Nobles Farm go right over a stile and left to join the drive from the cottage which you can follow for over $\frac{1}{4}$ mile out to a road.

⑤ Turn left beneath the railway and after less than 100 yards go right along a track to a stile, then squarely ahead across the middle of a large field. At the far end go ahead over a stile and ahead on a wide track. On approaching buildings go half left to a stile and right round two sides of a field until you can go right over a stile and

PLACES OF INTEREST NEARBY

The **Bluebell Railway** operates vintage steam trains along a 10-mile stretch of restored railway between Sheffield Park and Kingscote with an intermediate stop at Horsted Keynes. It is open daily from May to September and every weekend at school half term. Telephone: 01825 720800 for train times.

East Grinstead
The Old Mill

| **MAP:** OS EXPLORER 135 (GR 392368) | **WALK 30** | **DISTANCE:** 3½ MILES |

DIRECTIONS TO START: DUNNINGS MILL, ON THE SOUTHERN OUTSKIRTS OF THE TOWN, IS BEST APPROACHED FROM A ROUNDABOUT ON THE B2110 TURNERS HILL ROAD VIA HURST FARM ROAD, THEN RIGHT ALONG DUNNINGS ROAD. **PARKING:** YOU ARE WELCOME TO PARK IN THE LARGE CAR PARK BEHIND THE PUB, SHARED WITH THE NEIGHBOURING LEISURE AND SOCIAL CENTRES.

Well placed as a starting point for a walk, on the southern edge of the town of East Grinstead, you are soon in quiet countryside on a gently undulating route through woods and meadows and passing close to Standen House (see Places of Interest Nearby). A descent past an area of sandstone outcrops within an open access area established under the Countryside Stewardship Scheme at Standen Rocks brings you to the edge of the large Weir Wood Reservoir. The return route offers a fairly direct path through alternating woods and fields, ending along a quiet streamside path at the edge of the town.

The Old Mill

Housed in what was once a water mill, built in the 17th century, the Old Mill, formerly know as Dunnings Mill, was converted into a pub in the 1940s. It is large rambling place, full of character, incorporating four bars on four different levels as well as a restaurant extension built over the old mill stream with a view of the original mill wheel from the back window. In the summer you can sit outside on a brick patio or on one of the lawns at the side and rear of the premises. The Old Mill is a Harveys Brewery pub, held on a tenancy and, not surprisingly, serves Harveys Sussex Ale, supplemented by rotating seasonal ales from the same Lewes brewery and drawn straight from a cask in the pub cellar. The bar menu offers sandwiches with wholemeal or ciabatta bread. More elaborate restaurant fare is, however, available to bar customers and includes a wide choice of home-made puddings.

The opening times are from 11 am to 11 pm on Monday to Saturday and 12 noon to 10.30 pm on Sunday. Food is served from 12 noon to 2.30 pm and 6 pm to 9.30 pm Monday to Friday (all day on Saturday and Sunday). Children and dogs are welcome. Telephone: 01342 326341.

The Walk

① From the pub turn right and, after about 150 yards, go right again along Combe Hill Road. After another 200 yards turn left along a metalled drive, waymarked as part of the High Weald Landscape Trail which you will be following as far as the reservoir. Where

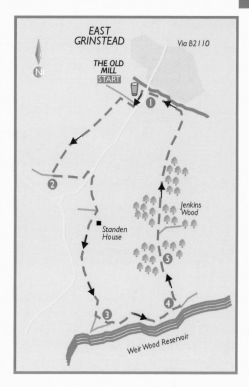

the drive ends, a path continues through five meadows. In the last of these a signpost directs you into an enclosed path along the right edge of the field.

② Both paths lead to a junction where you should turn left along the left edge of a playing field and out to a road. Turn left and shortly go right along the drive to Standen. After about 300 yards turn right along an enclosed path, still marked with the Landscape Trail logo. Beyond a kissing gate the path drops down along the left edge of a field with a glimpse of the reservoir ahead. Towards the bottom corner of the field go ahead along an enclosed path, ignoring signed paths to left and right. Follow a fence, left, down between wooded banks to enter the

Weir Wood Reservoir

Countryside Stewardship area of Standen Rocks. Shortly where you have a choice of signed paths, either will do. Both take you down to the edge of the Weir Wood Reservoir.

③ Turn left along the reservoir perimeter path, parting company with the High Weald Trail which goes off to the right but joining, for a short distance, the Sussex Border Path. Follow the tiresome reservoir fence, partly enclosed, partly open on your left, for over $\frac{1}{4}$ mile, ignoring the first stiled and signed path to the left.

④ At a three-armed signpost at the far end of a meadow, open to your left, turn left along a right field edge, through a gap and across the next field, passing to the right of an electricity pylon. Cross a stile and continue parallel to the left edge of two fields with a stile between them, in the second field skirting to the right of a picturesque pond.

⑤ From the second field corner go forward through a small wood, on across a field and down through a larger area of woodland where you should ignore a signed path to the left. Cross a stream, leave the wood and keep to the right of the field beyond. Carry on through another belt of woodland and down across two more fields. At the bottom of the hill go through a bridle gate into a wood and immediately turn left along a path within the wood edge. Follow this well-trodden path on and out through a recreation ground to reach the road opposite the pub.

PLACES OF INTEREST NEARBY

Standen House (National Trust) was built in 1890 and is notable for its internal decoration by William Morris, including carpets and original wallpapers. The beautiful garden overlooks the rolling well-wooded countryside explored on the walk. House and garden are open from the end of March to the beginning of November, Wednesday to Sunday. Telephone: 01342 323029.